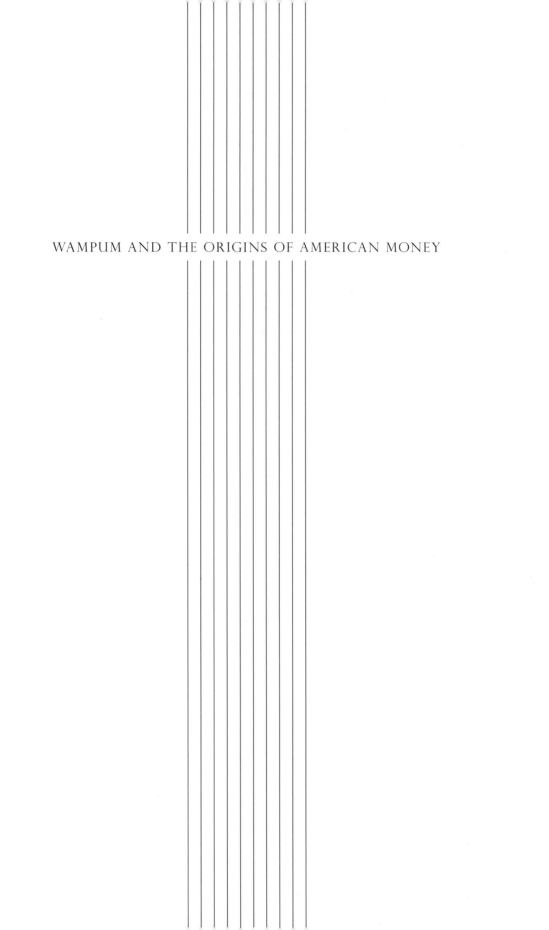

WAMPUM AND THE ORIGINS OF AMERICAN MONEY

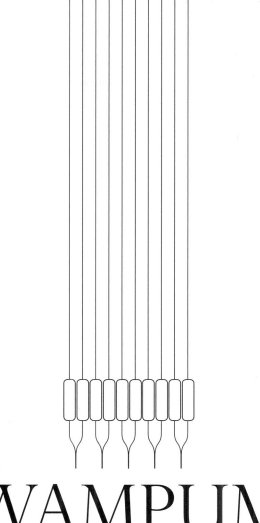

WAMPUM

and the Origins of American Money

Marc Shell

University of Illinois Press
Urbana, Chicago, and Springfield

For Susan

CONTENTS

Color plates follow page 46

ILLUSTRATIONS

Figures

Plates

Following page 46

ABBREVIATIONS

AFC	Oscar G. Schilke and Solomon Schilke, *America's Foreign Coins: An Illustrated Standard Catalogue with Valuations of Foreign Coins with Legal Tender Status in the United States, 1793–1857* (New York: Coin and Currency Institute, 1964).
ANS	American Numismatic Society, New York, New York
Beauchamp	William Martin Beauchamp, *Wampum and Shell Articles used by the New York Indians* (Albany: University of the State of New York, 1901).
CS	Collection Selechonek, Grand Manan Island, New Brunswick
Durand	Roger H. Durand, *Some Interesting Notes about Indians* (Rehoboth, Mass.: Durand and Co., 1991).
Eckstorm	Fannie Hardy Eckstorm, *Old John Neptune and Other Maine Indian Shamans* (Portland, Me.: Southworth-Anthoensen Press, 1945).
HCL	Harvard College Library, Cambridge, Massachusetts.
HMS	*The Herb and Martha Schingoethe Obsolete Currency Collection.* Part 3. Memphis International Auction. June 17 and 18, 2005 (New York: Smythe, 2005).
Low	Lyman Haynes Low, *Hard Time Tokens.* 1899. Reprint: introd. Edward Janis (New York: Sanford J. Durst, 1977).
Newman	Eric P. Newman, *The Early Paper Money of America,* 3rd ed. (Iola, Wisc.: Krause, 1990).
Oreshnikov	Alekse Vasilevich Oreshnikov, *Russkiia monety do 1547 goda* (Moscow: T-vo Tip. A. I. Mamontova, 1896).
Petrov	Vasili Il'ich Petrov, *Catalogue des monnaies russes de tous les princes, tsars et empereurs depuis 980 jusqu'à 1899* (1899; reprint, Graz: Akademische Druck-u. Verlagsantstalt, 1964).
Rulau	Russell Rulau, *Hard Times Tokens, 1832–1844. A Complete Revision and Enlargement of Lyman H. Low's 1899 Classic Reference,* 4th ed. (Iola, Wisc.: Krause, 1992). Illustrations are from the edition of 1899.
Wells	David Ames Wells, *Robinson Crusoe's Money; or, The Remarkable Financial Fortunes and Misfortunes of a Remote Island Community,* illus. Thomas Nast (New York: Harper, 1876).

ACKNOWLEDGMENTS

Many groups and persons helped with the work at hand. I am grateful to the Ouje-Bougoumou (Cree) at Chabougamau and the Mohawk (Iroquois) at Kanasetake and Lac des Deux Montagnes, Québec, with whom I spent much time in the 1950s and 1960s. I thank especially all those scholars of Native American and First Nation languages who helped me with issues of translation and transcription. They made me quite aware of what I do not know (and maybe cannot know) by way of language.

I have sought and received the help of many generous persons and institutions. Among these are the many colleagues and specialists in Canada and the United States who have provided invaluable assistance and historical insight. Students of Harvard College in Cambridge (Massachusetts), Cascais (Portugal), and Olympia (Greece) contributed in myriad ways. My lectures on the subject of wampum in several venues—including Irvine, California, and Harvard University's Native American Program—prompted excellent questions and observations. Casiana Ionita helped with research problems involving permissions and illustrations. Eli Ewing, a Cherokee at Harvard Law School, provided encouragement and support with language. I also thank Frederick Hoxie, who commented brilliantly on the manuscript; Jonathan C. Lainey, for excellent research advice on wampum belts still in Québec; and Eric Schena, for superb scholarly leads on bilingual dengas.

I am thankful to the Harvard University Libraries for generous assistance with books, manuscripts, and visual materials. For books printed in Montréal, Sorel, Sillery, Ottawa, Québec City, Fredericton, and elsewhere in the Maritime Provinces of Canada, I am indebted to the libraries at Université de Montréal, McGill University (Montréal), Université de Moncton (Moncton), and the University of New Brunswick (Fredericton).

Institutions generously made photographs and other visual materials available. In Canada there are the Archives and Research Library of the New Brunswick Museum (Saint John, New Brunswick), Communications New Brunswick (Fredericton), Electric Studio (Brantford, Ontario), Micmac-Maliseet Institute (New Brunswick), McCord Museum (Montréal), Musée de la civilisation (Archives du Séminaire de Québec), National Archives of Canada (Ottawa), and Public Archives of Canada (Ottawa).

In the United States there are the American Topical Association (Arlington, Texas), American Numismatic Society (New York City), C. E. Smith Museum of Anthropology (California State University at Hayward), and Collection Selechonek (Grand Manan Island, New Brunswick). There are also the Library of Congress (Washington, D.C.), Lilly Library (Indiana University),

Massachusetts Historical Society (Boston), National Museum of the American Indian (Smithsonian Institution, Washington, D.C.), George Gustav Heye Center (New York City), Society of Paper Money Collectors (Chapel Hill, North Carolina), and the Six Nations Indian Museum (Onchiota, New York). Museums elsewhere that assisted include the Vatican Museums (Rome, Italy). Among individuals who provided materials and helped in many other ways are Lisa Brooks (scholar), Roger H. Durand (numismatist), Idra Labrie (photographer), and Karen Yxomme Lynch Harley (artist).

To family and friends, and especially Susan Shell and Werner Sollors, I am eternally grateful.

It was not only my personal experience in Québec that encouraged me to dare working in this area. Some of my earlier intellectual work and research encouraged me to try writing about wampum.

First was my study of money and language as media of representation and exchange. I wrote about political and cultural aspects of the introduction of coined money in ancient Greece in *The Economy of Literature* (1978), which focuses on questions of tyranny and philosophy as well as laws of purchase and sale. In *Money, Language, and Thought* (1982), I extended this analysis both to credit money in Europe and—more pertinent—to the fiduciary and political experiments in the northern part of North America that became the United States. Later on, in *Art and Money* (1994), I explored several questions involving economic fetishism and religion in the aesthetic realm, again with special attention to the United States. In *The Painting in the Trash Bin* (forthcoming), I take up the work of the German-American counterfeiter and artist Otis Kaye, who painted various trompe l'oeil money works and, in that context, treated the question of the American Indian.

The second broad area of my research concerned the sociology of language. This area has had four interrelated foci. First is bilingualism in the sphere of commercial advertising, with semiotic forays—including an essay entitled "La Publicité bilingue au Québec" in the *Journal Canadien de Recherche Sémiotique* (1977)—into specifically Canadian aspects of the interrelationship between language and money. Second is the history of the non-English languages and literatures in what is now the United States, which I explored in a book, *American Babel,* with the overconfident subtitle *Literatures of the United States from Abnaki to Zuni* (2002). In such work, I have tried to define the limits of knowledge imposed by the lack of extant written and oral materials and also to recover something of the effect of hearing unrecognized languages, as in *Stutter* (2006). Third is literary relations between the United States and French Canada, including the *métis,* the subject of a short work, *French-Canadian/American Literary Relations* (1967), published at the French Canada Studies Institute at McGill University. Fourth is group identity in relationship to language wars, including, in *Children of the Earth* (1994), European notions of group identity as they involve both imperialism and genocide.

For all those who encouraged this work, thanks.

WAMPUM AND THE ORIGINS OF AMERICAN MONEY

INTRODUCTION

Why Wampum?

THE BELT OF WAMPUM,
AND THE COMMERCE OF AMERICA,
ARE ALIKE.

——RALPH WALDO EMERSON,
"THE POET" (1844)

Commercial exchange really matters to civilizations and how they change. For example, when the Greek cultures encountered those of Asia Minor in the sixth century B.C., there came along a new medium of monetary representation (coinage). The advent of this novel medium paralleled the beginnings of innovative forms of linguistic representation (philosophy) and the development of a new and disturbing kind of political representation (tyranny).[1] *Nomismos* is the key term for understanding the momentous change in the Classical world; nowadays we have come to understand it partly in terms of conventional coin (*nummus*). Something like the same historical transition in the realms of economics, language, and political power took place when the "Old World" (Great Britain and Europe) and the "New World" (Native America) encountered each other beginning in the sixteenth century. For understanding this transformation, the key term would be *wampum*. Defining wampum as such is the business of the present book.

Wampum focuses on "Indian and white ingenuity," taken together.[2] British and European settlers and invaders came to the northeastern part of North America with their own various notions about economic and linguistic exchange. Once there, they *adopted* the local currencies. Within a few years, they were also *adapting* those currencies according to their own traditional practices. Each national group—Dutch, French, English[3]—did so according to its own past experience and also according to the various practices of the tribes it met—Wampanoag, Mohawk, Iroquois.[4] Until around 1700, wampum per se often served "as currency for the North American Indians both among themselves and in dealings with Europeans; also, in *early colonial times, between Europeans* for the payment of small amounts."[5] Thereafter, wampum, transformed, gradually became the currency of America and, as it were, its actual politics.

The visual arts, numismatic evidence, literature, philosophizing, religious tracts, and diplomacy of the American colonies, and later of the United States, show that the settlers had subtle and intelligent ways of expressing their own assimilation of Indian trading practices. Likewise, they had productive ways of both articulating and repressing their fears that they were "becoming Indians." In the strictly political realm, American experimentation with what many called "paper wampum" began in 1690. That is the year when paper banknotes, showing Indian insignia, first came to the fore. Ever afterward the new medium—widespread paper money—uniquely informed American colonial life. Eventually, it both fueled and defined the (liberal) American republic.

Several scholars in the late nineteenth century properly argued that the British and European use of wampum in the New World was a main articulating influence for understanding the novel civilization of America. William Weeden's delicately entitled *Indian Money as a Factor in New England Civilization* (1884), for example, was even one of the earliest official "university press" books in the United States.[6] Together with several works published during the next two decades—including Alexander Del Mar's *History of Money in America* (1899)[7]—*Indian Money* ought to have set the pace for understanding the vital, distinctive American numismatic history. By the twentieth century, however, most historians of American money were getting nervous when the time came for them to discuss wampum. Many passed over wampum by means of awkward silence, or by telling an off-putting joke or two, or by reporting a good-humored, sidetracking anecdote. Each national group had its favorite distracting tales. Many French Canadian historians, for example, liked to repeat the story about how Jacques Cartier, the sixteenth-century explorer, believed that wampum was as good for stopping nosebleeds as for money.[8] All such rhetorical strategies for avoiding discussion of how wampum might have mattered, to the economic and cultural history of North America, made the Indian pay again through the nose.

Certain factors always at work in the United States may shed a little light on why Americans of the last century avoided discussing wampum seriously; the same factors may also serve to introduce why the issue of wampum needs revisiting—and how. For example, a few twentieth-century historians seem to avoid the issue of Indian money because they have a "guilty conscience" about the genocide of the Indians. After the battles of Little Big Horn (1886) and Wounded Knee (1890), that would be psychologically understandable. Other historians, similarly disturbed by American history, are worried how sustained attention to wampum might unsettle comfortable notions of national ownership. For every satisfying story about the fair purchase of Manhattan Island from the Wappinger by the Dutchman Peter Minuit in 1626, for example, there is a matching history about "the [wampum] beads that did *not* buy Manhattan Island" (italics mine).[9] General George Crook—the all-American Indian-fighter—said that "greed and avarice on the part of the Whites, in other words, the Almighty Dollar, is at the bottom of nine tenths of all our Indian troubles."[10] That Americans live in "the home of the brave" (as "The Star Spangled Banner" [1814] has it) makes some people fearful of revisiting, even on the merely *ideal* plane, what was the wampum that purchased national *real* estate.

One intellectually disconcerting reason that helps explain the twentieth-century dearth of information about wampum, and even of informed interest in wampum, has to do with the early twentieth-century demise of the field of comparative numismatics. Numismatics as such dealt with particular, or culturally specific, fiduciary grammars and their material articulations, including those of the native cultures of the northeast part of North America. Early twentieth-century social science, however, wanted a "culture-neutral" economic science. It aimed at immediate, and sometimes plainly mathematical, transcendence of culturally specific particularities. The First World War gave impetus to such universalist science, since it seemed to arise from nationally specific economic and culturally particular interests. At around this time, most all numismatic objects—shells and wampum belts, coins, banknotes, bank records, treaties, drawings, photographs, recordings—became private collectors' items and museum pieces, or they were discarded or disassembled as junk. Numismatic writings found their way onto the backroom library shelves, where they have mostly remained now for a century.

During precisely the same decades, Americans were turning against the study, and even the use, of all particular languages and writing systems except English and the Roman alphabet. This change too had drastic effects on the study of wampum. First, wampum was understood as a "language," along with drum and sign language, and so it was relegated to the dustbin of history. Second, knowledge of Native American languages is really needed in order to understand what wampum was and what it had become. Third, a great many indigenous languages and economic cultures had already been annihilated anyway, and many more remained with hardly a trace. The American turn against languages exacerbated this linguicide.

The consequent difficulties for scholarship are familiar to Classical scholars. As always, the best is the enemy of the good. Scholars of comparative literature and researchers in comparative numismatics know quite well some of the relevant systems of language and banking; if they also become intelligently aware of what they don't know well, then they are able to deal well enough with what they know only imperfectly.

The opening chapters of this book deal with a larger history of money, language, and thought that builds a reliable framework for the study of wampum. These chapters discuss the role of a monetary lingua franca in a country without an official language. They focus on "foreign legal tender" and "bilingual coinage." They touch on theoretical problems involving meaning and value, with special attention to counterfeiting, state money, and local notions of debt or credit.

In the middle chapters I discuss definitions and historiographies of wampum. Special consideration is given to Indian writing and diplomacy and to settlers' uses and transformations of wampum. We shall see here that the American reworking of wampum was sometimes overlooked by scholars because of a long-standing twentieth-century predisposition to think about money and language as entirely discrete categories or to believe that money and art are absolutely different entities.

The last chapters focus on the American linguistic and political highway that starts with wampum and seems to end with Wall Street. The main way station is the American Revolution itself. Wampum transformed does not constitute a full system of letters patent.[11] Nor is the North American monetary and linguistic experience unique in all respects.[12] And yet, pluralist interaction between indigenous and European exchange systems, both linguistic and monetary, helped make for the cultural and political foundation of North America as we know it.

This is a little book that lays out a now relatively new subject rather than trying to exhaust an old subject. It tells only part of the story of Indian money in America, but it is a part that indicates the whole. The book's references and notes are guideposts to further reading and research. One model for this sort of book is Marc Bloch's *Sketch of a Monetary History of Europe*.[13] The *Sketch* tells a small part of the story of European money while suggesting a whole that is unfolding, these days, in the shape of the European Union. A discussion of the Union of European States, which lays out some of the central linguistic and monetary concerns of old-fashioned nation-states, is where the first chapter of *Wampum* begins the present discussion of the United States of America.

CHAPTER ONE

Money and Language

JUST AS IN AN HISTORICAL LABYRINTH,
THE GRAMMATICAL STRUCTURE
OF A LANGUAGE IS A MUCH SAFER GUIDE
THAN THE MERE SIMILARITY OF LETTERS
OR SOUNDS, SO IS THE STRUCTURE
OF A MONETARY SYSTEM, AS COMPARED
WITH MERE TYPES OF COINS.

—ALEXANDER DEL MAR

"Money speaks sense in a Language all Nations understand," wrote Aphra Behn in her play *The Rover* (1681).[1] This statement is attractive insofar as it seems to go beyond saying "All human beings alike are venal" and suggests that "money talk," whatever that is, might be a solution to problems of translingual, international communication. Behn's statement gains this attractiveness, however, only by passing over issues of elementary import. Perhaps not all nations have money. Maybe the monetary systems of nations vary from people to people in the same way that languages vary. If so, is the language that Behn's money speaks comprehensibly to all nations one of many such universal languages—a sort of lingua franca?

Alternatively, is money the only universal language—a sort of Pentecostal glossalalia? In nineteenth-century America, such questions were already posed in terms of wampum. Gilbert Parker writes in *Mrs. Falchion* (1893) that the main trade languages of the New World mediated among different spoken languages in the same way that wampum, itself already a linguistic as well as economic medium, mediated among different fiduciary systems. "These strange old hymns were written in Chinook, that strange [trading] language—French, English, Spanish,

Indian, arranged by the Hudson's Bay Company, which is, like the wampum belt, a common tongue for the tribes and peoples not speaking any language but their own."[2]

Babel

Economists and monetary geographers, in order to discuss money in universalist terms, often come to rely on the rhetoric of "the one and the many" presupposed by the biblical story of the tower of Babel. Frequently, political economists even refer to a curt statement by John Stuart Mill in his influential *Principles of Political Economy, with Some of Their Applications to Social Philosophy* (1848). Mill writes that the existence of "a multiplicity of national moneys," which situation he bemoans, is a barbarism: "So much of barbarism, however, still remains in the transactions of most civilized nations, that almost all independent countries choose to assert their nationality by having, to their own inconvenience and that of their neighbours, a peculiar currency of their own."[3] The term *barbarian* usually denotes one who does not know *our* language, and it often comes to denote savages who do not know *any* language. (Further, insofar as we may not know another person's manner of talking, we will sometimes be unable to recognize a foreigner's apparent babbling as a human language.) So Mill's term, *barbarism*—which qualifies shibboleth-like the peoples, including even "civilized nations," who are unable to speak our language—already contains the germinal nostalgia for a single language of yore: the pre-Babel universal language. By way of analogy, the Indian term *Wyandot,* by which the Huron nations of the northeast part of North America called themselves, means "people of one speech."[4]

For economists in the tradition of Mill's "social philosophy," there are usually two interrelated dialectics silently (and often also uncritically) at work in their "geography of money." First is the rhetorical dialectic of the one and the many. Second is the tension between two polar-opposite notions lurking behind this idea of the one. On the one pole is the view that there should be one currency for a nation: "One nation, one currency" is the relevant rallying cry. On the other pole is the view that there should be one currency in the world: "One world, one currency" is the appropriate motto. The hypothesis of one currency, whether global or national, supposes potentially two apparently different political ends: the existence of many nations, each one with its own currency; and the destruction of all nations except one. If those who yearn for the pre-Babel language generally have a more or less imperialist yen for plural linguicides, those who crave one world currency for the future usually want what I call "nummicides."[5]

Debates about European "monetary union" in the last century clarify the operation of this dialectic. On one side of the debate are the arguments that the foundation of each nation-state is intimately and inextricably linked with its own currency. Hoffman says, "Most independent nations—except for a few that belong to currency unions—continue to issue their own currencies and use them within their borders."[6] Hirsch, interpreting the trendsetting Treaty of Westphalia (1648), writes, "One of the hallmarks of national sovereignty through the ages has been the right to create money. . . . The ability to create its own domestic money is the key financial distinction of a sovereign state."[7] (The Treaty of Westphalia was the foundational agreement be-

1. Photograph of Alexander Del Mar, 1868. CS.

tween the Holy Roman Emperor and the King of France, along with their respective allies.)[8] Michael Mussa, considering work at the European Monetary Union, wrote similarly that "virtually all the world's nations assert and express their sovereign authority by maintaining a distinct national money and protecting its use within respective jurisdictions. Money is like a flag; each country has to have its own."[9] On the other side of the debate, there are those economists who see nothing special in a nation's *not* having its own currency. Fischer writes, "There is nothing especially exotic about an economy that does not use its own money."[10] Pascal Salin writes similarly, "The production of money, like the production of law, is not an essential attribute of state sovereignty, despite what the mythology says."[11]

Behind all such would-be demythologizing statements about nationhood and money, there often lurk oversimplifications—probably rhetorically necessary in such disputes. In fact, a surprising number of economists seem to agree explicitly with Harmelink that a nation is merely "a people with a common confusion as to their origins and a common antipathy to their neighbors."[12] When one is armed with this simple credo, it is almost effortless to believe, as many economists do, that all that would be needed for world peace is a universal currency system. Such a system would mark "the end of [national] geography."[13] The new "de-territorialized" currency, say its sponsors, will now "promote a different sense of identity," and presumably a much better one.[14]

There are problems with this hypothetical notion of a numismatic Pax Romana. First is the likelihood of the terrible genocides that any such *pax* seems almost to presuppose as a foundational prerequisite. Moreover, as Alexander Del Mar (fig. 1) pointed out already in the 1890s, the actual (i.e., historical) Pax Romana required a bimetallic standard: gold for imperial Rome and silver for the colonies.[15] Second is the list of venal reasons why a sovereign—of whatever national stripe—should want to control his or her own coinage. Not the least of these reasons is the *seignorage,* or "the excess of the nominal value of a currency over its cost of production."[16]

The notion that statehood and a single monetary system are extricable brings us also to the arguments of those money geographers who, like Boyer-Xambeu, claim that before the nineteenth century, the rule of thumb was that "coins circulated everywhere without consideration for frontiers."[17] This claim disregards several factors that the careful numismatists of the nineteenth century would not have overlooked. One is the difference between fiduciary and nonfiduciary coin. Another is the difference between foreign tender and foreign *legal* tender. Only the latter circulates with legal status thanks to national "pegging" of its rate; the former is not pegged but instead circulates as a regular commodity.[18] The claim that coin circulates without regard to frontiers thus involves us in questions of foreign tender, both legal and not.

Political Economy

In the nation-state we call the United States, many languages other than American English once circulated (together with American English). This widespread presence of "foreign" languages, which some observers have called "peculiar," was due partly to the condition that there was no official language or languages in the United States. The parallel situation in the monetary realm was this: for the first four score and seven years, the United States had no single official national currency. From the start, Webster's great American dictionary was therefore careful to include both word definitions and money conversions. At the time of the Civil War, the linguistic history of the United States diverged from its monetary history; now there would be a single official currency (no more foreign legal tender). Nowadays there is still not an official language in the United States, but there is an official currency. The divergence tends to obscure the formative and still informing cultural conditions of the United States during those four score and seven years to which Lincoln refers.

By the eighteenth century, people had already long taken a single money standard and a single language to be the twin signs of nation-statehood. Consider here what European scholars used to call the monetary conditions of such "city-statehood" as that in ancient Greece. The same might be said for language, especially after the fall of such pluralist political institutions as the Ottoman Empire, the Hapsburg Empire, and the new European Union. One way to set out discussion of the homology between money and language involves defining the various "syntaxes" of money and then showing in what ways nationally different banking systems coexisted.

Scrutinizing the supposed "material basis" of currency systems (gold, silver, bronze, and shell) is the business of comparative numismatics, an old-time precursor to what we now sometimes call the study of material culture in the monetary realm. These days, however, we are at a disadvantage in treating the languages of money, especially in the New World, where so many different indigenous Indian groups and European nations traded with one another. We are at a disadvantage because a numismatics that heeds cultural specificities has played a relatively minor role in the social sciences and humanities for at least a century. Nowadays, numismatics interests many coin collectors and dealers but only a few historians, archeologists, and art historians.

What happened to numismatics? One answer helps to explain why wampum—the subject of the present inquiry and itself the subject of much serious nineteenth-century numismatics—has largely disappeared from public inquiry. We moderns and postmoderns have given up culturally *particular* numismatics, though not so much because we eschew the realm of the antiquarian (though we often do that). Mainly, in the decades before the First World War, we fell under the spell of those *universalist* doctrines—including the policy or theory that identifies itself as value-neutral and absolutely nontotemic—that wanted to put out of mind the intellectually difficult and the politically threatening *specificities* that actual numismatics incessantly places before us. Comparative numismatics was once an excellent guide to the particular socio- and psychopathological aspects of monetary practices and policies.

In fact, it was from numismatic investigation in the New World in particular that the European languages and cultures got such sociologically diagnostic terms as *totem*. This Ojibwa word means something like "mark" or armorial "bearing"[19] and has important implications for anthropological and psychoanalytic interpretations of *nomos* and *nomismos*—or of "social convention" and "fetishes in exchange." The Canadian educator John George Hodgins writes in his influential *History of Canada* (1866), "The totem, or outline of some animal (from *do-daim,* a family mark), was always the chief's signature to a treaty."[20] Oliphant suggested (1887) that certain ideas of authorizing, political "signature" unite here the notion of language and money.[21] James George Frazer's definition of *totem* in the *Encyclopaedia Britannica* (1911) seems relevant here: "A totem is a class of material objects which a *savage* regards with superstitious respect, believing that there exists between him and every member of the class an intimate and altogether special relation."[22] The definition seems to bring to bear the ancient European struggle between iconoclasm and iconodulism, with all its freighted notions about idolatry. We will consider later the needful questions, Who is the savage here? and Who the civilized person?—or, as the apportioning judge from Belmont asks in Shakespeare's play *The Merchant of Venice,* "Which is the merchant here, and which the Jew?"[23]

The new faith in "civilized" universalism, which triggered or accompanied the demise of particularized scientific numismatics in the early years of the twentieth century, has had many a latter-day spokesperson. Among them would be the hypercivilized econometrist Paul Samuelson. He argued that mathematics is a language, meaning that monetary policy could be universal, neutral, and value-free.[24] There are some problems with this position. When would-be value-neutral economists invoke the comparison between mathematics and language, they usually presume that mathematics is logically precedent, hence also superior, to all other languages, in much the same way that some religious scholars might say that the pre-Babel language or apocalyptic Pentecostalism is better than the babbling confusions that followed. In fact, the more appropriate parallel between money and language would be drawn between monetary systems and linguistic systems. Money is not a language in the same way that French or Ojibwa is a language, but the French or Ojibwa monetary scheme is akin to the French language or the Ojibwa language. Likewise, one might say that language itself (which includes that of speakers of French and Ojibwa) is like money itself (which includes that used by French and Ojibwa traders).

At just the time of the ideological turn against numismatics, Alexander Del Mar was exploring precisely this link between comparative monetary systems and comparative language. An econometrician and multilingual American scholar of Algerian descent who founded what became the Internal Revenue Service of the United States, Del Mar wrote the following about the link, especially in America, between money and language: "the grammatical structure of a language" is like "the structure of a monetary system."[25] Del Mar's call for multilingual numismatic literacy, for which he argues in several key books on the subject, has to do mainly with nations in relationship to linguistic and cultural production and exchange. It looks to understanding the cultural economics of the United States in terms of its reliance on wampum and paper money in the seventeenth and eighteenth centuries, which reliance led up to the American Revolution. And, as we shall see in the case of the American credit economy, it also allows access to understanding the cultural implications of American reliance on foreign legal tender, which began with the official use of wampum in the seventeenth century and flourished in the nineteenth century until the Civil War.

CHAPTER TWO

Foreign Legal Tender

COINAGE IS PECULIARLY AN
ATTRIBUTE OF SOVEREIGNTY.
TO TRANSFER ITS EXERCISE TO
ANOTHER COUNTRY, IS TO SUBMIT
IT TO ANOTHER SOVEREIGN.

——THOMAS JEFFERSON,
U.S. SECRETARY OF STATE,
COINAGE REPORT (1790)

At certain times in its history, the United States has been the most widely polyglot place on earth. (Henry James bemoans that condition when he observes immigrants in New York City.) This condition included America's having plenty of "foreign tender." Coins—the most widely circulated printed literature—came from within and without the political borders of what we now call the United States. In the colonial period, much of this foreign tender circulated more or less as a commodity. We are concerned here, however, only with that foreign tender whose circulation, within the borders of the United States, was mandated by law.[1]

I distinguish this foreign legal tender from coin struck by United States mints and sold to various foreign countries as their legal tender as well as from coins struck at foreign mints at the behest of the United States and with the insignia of the United States.[2]

That there were American coins struck at foreign mints was not a happy circumstance for everyone. Thomas Jefferson, for one, said that a country, in order to be a real country, must have a mint of its own.[3] And many U.S. secretaries of the treasury often suggested that there was some reason to distrust foreign coin.[4] The consequent debate involves the parallel question

whether a nation-state needs its own dictionary, grammar, or national linguistic academy
in order to be a real nation-state.

People are sometimes surprised to learn
of official American "monetary multilingual-
ism." They wonder at the condition where a
country's treasury recognizes, as its own legal
tender, coins from other countries that bear
only the official seals of those other countries.
There are mitigating circumstances, of course.
First, the United States is not alone among
the nations in having foreign legal tender.[5]
Second, the plentiful multiplicity of (official
mandated) foreign legal tender in the United
States between the Revolutionary and Civil
Wars matches the multiplicity of (unofficial)
languages. In 1776, only 38 percent of people
in the American colonies were anglophone.

2. Coin. Portugal. 1822. John VI, King of
Portugal and Brazil. "Joe" is the abbreviation
or nickname of Joannes or Johannes.
ANS 1001.1.25867.

Congress has never made English, or any other language, the official language of the United
States—a distinguishing though not unique factor of American law.

Third, the lexical marks of past monetary regimes suffuse the American language as virtually
none other. The terms are hard to miss. Hundreds of such words inform America's "shell-game"
lingo of money. Consider the English-language words *medio, two bits,* and *joe,* all of which refer to
actual coins that were pegged at definite values and circulated by law (fig. 2).[6] There is likewise
the *shilling, escudo,* and *real* (fig. 3).[7] The word *dollar* is "foreign," and foreign too is the *pillar
dollar* and the visual sign for the dollar ($) (fig. 4).[8] The money term *clam* is apparently Native
American and often means "dollar" (plate 1). *Clam* recalls bead or shell money (fig. 5)—that
is, wampum.[9] The multiplicity of such terms still betokens that there was foreign coin in the
United States.

Much of that foreign coin was legal tender. Of the $23,000,000 circulating as legal tender
in coin in the United States in 1830, $9,000,000 was in foreign coin. These foreign coins were
not always of small denomination. For example, the Portuguese 20,000 *reis* coin (fig. 6) was
foreign legal tender and would be worth well over $32 in 1814.[10]

Why was there so much foreign coin? From 1789 to 1864, specie was rare in the United
States, partly because American coins were hoarded abroad. In fact, not until 1853—two years
after the publication of *Moby-Dick; or, The Whale,* with its well-known equatorial doubloon—did
the United States produce "fiduciary" coins, that is, coins worth "intrinsically" less than their
face values.[11] The long-standing American production of only nonfiduciary coins seems to represent a typically naïve appreciation of specie. That apparent naïveté needs to be understood
in terms of the advanced and sophisticated American pattern of using paper money as early as

3. Coin. Mexico. Eight reales. 1824. Eagle devouring snake. "Hook-necked" eagle facing left. Reverse: Liberty cap, rays, and date. *AFC* 371. ANS 1934.1.609.

4. Coin. Mexico. Eight reales. 1777. Charles III appears on the obverse. ANS 1934.1.565. From Raphael E. Solomon, "Foreign Coins in America," in *Studies on Money in Early America,* ed. Eric P. Newman and Richard Doty (New York: American Numismatic Society, 1976), 40.

the colonial period, a point I take up later.[12] In any case, the shortage of government-issued specie led to a great deal of private coinage and "hard times tokens."[13] More relevantly, it also led to the use of much unauthorized coinage in the United States. Among such coins would be the Chinese wen (fig. 7).[14]

The same specie shortage, together with the extraordinary bounty and opportunity of the New World, helps to explain why the United States legally allowed foreign coinage in quantities and at specific rates of monetary translation or conversion.

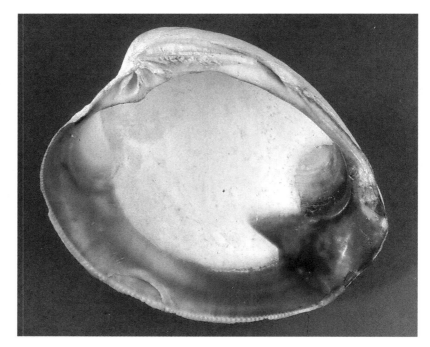

5. Quahog shell for making wampum. Nineteenth century. Photo courtesy
Peabody Museum of Archaeology and Ethnology, Harvard University.

7. Coin. China, Ch'ing Dynasty, Emperor
Ch'ien-lung. 1736–95. Commonly found in
North America. This example was found at a
site in Alexandria, Virginia. Photo courtesy
Alexandria Archaeology Museum, Alexandria,
Virginia.

6. Coin. Brazil. Twenty thousand reis. 1726.
Crowned arms of John V within inscription.
AFC 94. ANS 1945.42.819.

There are many examples of the foreign legal tender of the United States. Their types and inscriptions are widely circulating epigraphic poems and visual sculptures that a large part of the population both read and handled. Coins are the most widespread mechanically reproduced works of writing and imagery in the world, and when foreign, they demanded special cultural and linguistic preparedness.

British coins, of which the Americans used a great many, show the politically foundational imagery of Saint George killing the dragon (figs. 8, 9). Central American coins brilliantly conflate the sun with a coin (fig. 10), suggesting a relationship between natural wealth (the sun) and metallic wealth (the coin) that later comes to influence American money writers like David Wells and political cartoonists like Thomas Nast. A Peruvian coin of 1837 (fig. 11) probably inspired Melville in writing the famous "doubloon chapter" in *Moby-Dick; or, The Whale* (1851). Numismatic themes include preeminently the celebration of liberty and independence: the Chilean coins that show a condor breaking its chains (fig. 12) or an active volcano (fig. 13) and the French coins that celebrate "Liberty, Equality, Fraternity" (fig. 14). A French coin (1793) shows the act of writing the French constitution (fig. 15). Likewise, writing plays a role in a Mexican coin that circulated in the United States as foreign legal tender (fig. 16). Mexican tender that circulated in the United States by law often depicts such divine-right monarchs as King Charles IV of Spain. (The authorities in the United States were not always entirely pro-republican.)

Coin verses and obverses show consideration of the political aspects of coinage itself. Coins from Brazil (1833–40), for example, often include the numismatic inscription *In Hoc Signo*

8. Coin. Great Britain. Two pounds. 1823. Plain head of George IV. Reverse: Saint George slaying the dragon. *AFC* 160. ANS 1901.21.31.

9. Coin. Great Britain. One pound. 1817. Laureate head of George III.
Reverse: Saint George slaying the dragon. *AFC* 157. ANS 1905.57.429.

10. Coin. Guatemala. Eight reales. 1825. Sun behind mountain.
Reverse: tree in center divides value, 8 and R. *AFC* 160. ANS 1889.18.37.

11. Coin. Peru. Eight reales. 1837. REPUB SUD PERUANA. Sun and ray.
Reverse: CONFEDERACION. Castle, volcano. *AFC* 379. ANS 1920.100.2.

12. Coin. Chile. Eight reales. 1839–40. Condor
breaking chains. *AFC* 367. ANS 1934.1.453.

13. Coin. Chile. One peso. 1822. CHILE INDEPENDIENTE. Value above volcano.
Reverse: column surmounted by label inscribed LIBERTAD. *AFC* 162. ANS 0000.999.33915.

14. Coin. France. Twenty francs. 1850. Head of Ceres.
Reverse: LIBERTÉ, ÉGALITÉ, FRATERNITÉ. *AFC* 109. ANS 1984.87.1.

15. Coin. France. Six livres. 1793. Angel writing the constitution. *AFC* 105. ANS 1920.147.155.

16. Coin. Mexico. Eight escudos. 1823. "Hook-necked" eagle facing left.
Reverse: Liberty cap over book. *AFC* 314. ANS 1941.134.1.

Vinces (In this sign you will conquer]) (fig. 17). In such inscriptions, it is purposefully ambiguous whether the sign by which one conquers is the cross or the coin. *In Hoc Signo Vinces* already appeared on a coin issued by the Emperor Vetranio (c. A.D. 350) with a Victory crowning the Emperor Constantine, who holds a *labarum* bearing the Christian monogram. The inscription, a loose translation of the Greek legend *en touton nika* (By this conquer), is associated with Constantine's vision of the Flaming Cross before the Battle of the Milvian Bridge (A.D. 312)

17. Coin. Brazil. Ten thousand reis. 1836. Child head of Peter II. Reverse: IN HOC S[IGNO] VINCES (In this sign you will conquer), imperial arms. *AFC* 174. ANS 1952.58.2.

and hence recalls how Constantine became master of the Western Empire and its entire customhouse. One etymology of the American dollar sign claims that it is derived from Christian designs of *IHS* understood either as the acronymic abbreviation for *In Hoc Signo* or *Ihesus Hominem Salvator* (Jesus the savior of humanity) or as the first letters of the Greek spelling of *Jesus*. Such associations of coinage with Christ are both traditional and, as Jefferson knew, problematic.

In the New World, the Spanish king Philip II—who claimed to understand nothing about paper money in the Old World and its counterparts in the New World—established the first mint in the New World in Lima, Peru (1560s). Sometimes the old coins from the Spanish dominions and from Spain itself circulated as foreign legal tender in the United States (figs. 18–20).[15] Coins from the Spanish dominions (1772–89; 1732–46), including newer ones from Lima, show the Gates of Hercules. Coins showing these pillars had circulated for centuries in the New World.

The *columnario* (or pillar dollar) is often called the first universal coin. Thomas Jefferson had such a coin in mind when, on September 2, 1776, he recommended to the Continental Congress that the United States adopt the silver "Spanish Milled Dollar," called "Pillar Pieces of Eight," as the American monetary unit of value, and he wrote in the 1780s that the sign of the currency of the new United States should be familiar. Samuel Manning Welch suggests, in his *Recollections of Buffalo,* that the origin of the dollar sign—especially that with two vertical bars—involves Spanish or Mexican silver coins. This coin, Welch says, was "stamped on one side with what we suppose to be a representation of the pillars of Hercules, and from which came the typical or arbitrary sign of the dollar mark $, which some suppose to be a monogram of, or a gerrymandered U.S."[16]

18. Coin. Mexico. Four reales. 1735. Inscribed with name of Philip V.
Reverse: crowned shield of arms. *AFC* 382. ANS 0000.999.19797.

19. Coin. Mexico. Two reales. 1772. Bust of Charles III.
Reverse: crowned shield of arms. ANS 1934.1.565.

20. Coin. Spain. Twenty reales. 1850. New head of Isabella II.
Reverse: crowned shield of arms within the Order. *AFC* 460. ANS 1919.257.13.

After 1857, foreign coins no longer circulated in the United States as legal tender.[17] As I discussed in *The Economy of Literature* (1978), this was the same year that Melville published *The Confidence-Man*. That work includes an ironic metaphysics of Indian-hating, a canny theory of money as an "Archimedean power," and a definitive fascination with counterfeit detectors and money-conversion tables as the basis for numismatic and literary investigation.[18]

CHAPTER THREE

Translation and Conversion

THEIR OWNE [MONEY]
IS OF TWO SORTS.

——ROGER WILLIAMS,
*KEY INTO THE LANGUAGE
OF AMERICA* (1643)

Monies facilitate trade within one group and also between two or more groups. For some trad-ers—including especially money-changing merchants and bankers—numismatic handling came to require both linguistic translation and monetary conversion. Commercial transactions also demanded consideration of the relationship of both kinds of transfer to the purity and weight of the metal of the coins on which monetary inscriptions appear. Finally, they required study of the varyingly pegged values of these metals within several different state jurisdictions and in terms of the variable political powers of each of their supposedly legitimating authorities. For all these reasons, it should not be surprising that bilingual coinage should exist. The term *bilingual money* here means numismatic tokens impressed with alphabetic or other representa-tional symbols from two linguistically different cultures.

The first widespread bilingual coinage was issued in the region that consists of modern-day Afghanistan/Pakistan and northern India. Alexander the Great, a native Macedonian speaker who had been educated by the Greek-speaking Aristotle, issued these coins along with found-ing Indo-Greek city-states in that region. His partly experimental coinage deeply affected the cultures of the various Indian nations in terms of both religion and literature. For one thing,

21. Coin. Bactria. Tetradrachm. 170 B.C. Bust of Eukratides I. Bactria, a partly Hellenized country bordering India, had been part of Seleucid territory but gained its independence circa 250 B.C. Bactrian coins are known for strongly realistic portraits. © Copyright the Trustees of the British Museum.

Indian coins were the first to present life-like portraits of rulers (fig. 21). For another thing, the Greek coins were mini-sculptures as well as Greek statuary art or idols, so that the traditionally *abstract* representations on Indian money now became Greek-inspired *embodied* statuary. Many coins actually had a Greek god on the reverse and an Indian god on the obverse (fig. 22). Along these same lines, subsequent Indo-Greek coins were inscribed in bilingual format: on one side, there was Greek cursive script; on the other side, there was a language descended from Sanskrit, usually Brahmi or Karoshti. An example is the bronze rectangular bilingual hemi-obols struck at Pushkalavati during the rule of Eukratides I (170–145 B.C.) in Bactria.[1] The Kushan dynasty (beginning in A.D. 78) adopted the same bilingual practice even as it introduced the practice of putting an image of the ruler on coins. Examples include the coins of Vima Kadphises, which often had unusual material properties (they were magnets).

In the modern era, such bilingual coins—the first widespread, facing-page translations in history—still help us decipher ancient languages. The brilliant work of James Prinsep with the

22. Coin. Bactria. Gold dinar. A.D 100–126. Issued by Kanishka I (the Great). Obverse: king sacrificing at altar. Reverse: four-armed Shiva. © Copyright the Trustees of the British Museum.

Karoshti script on these bilingual coins (in 1838) was part of the same attempt to interpret the ancient world as Jean-François Champollion's solution to the translation problem of the Egyptian hieroglyphs on the Rosetta Stone (in 1822).[2] Sometimes, however, there were linguistic "deceptions" on the faces of such coins. One language or script was sometimes merely symbolic, for example, or the letters from an original numismatic legend were so crudely imitated from earlier coins that they became illegible. A bronze tetradrachm of Kujula Kadphises (circa A.D. 1–40) already has definitively pseudo-Greek characters on one side and real Karoshti writing on the other.[3] Deciphering such numismatic characters would be like trying to read the apparently iconic markings on American money today (eyes and pyramids, for example) as if they were genuinely comprehensible hieroglyphic or alphabetic writing.

Bilingual coinages besides those issued by the states of Alexander's empire include Arabic-language issues. First, bilingual Arabic coins issued in Muslim Spain in A.D. 716 bear the etymologically mysterious term *al-andalus* on them.[4] Second, coins minted by thirteenth- and fourteenth-century Cilician Armenian rulers display a varied bicultural iconography:[5] the issuing of bilingual coins (in Arabic and Armenian) emphasized relations with Muslim neighbors. Third, coins of Moscow are sometimes inscribed in Russian and Arabic, as in the coins issued by Dimitri Donskoi in the late fourteenth century (fig. 23) and then by his son Vasili I. There are also the bilingual coins of Ivan the Great, struck at a time of little Mongol interference. These read, "This is a *denga* of Moscow," repeated in Russian (fig. 24). The Moscow issues include pseudo-scripts. And coins released by Vasilii II Vasilievich ("the Blind") sometimes have *only* a pseudo-Arabic inscription on the reverse and no Russian inscription whatsoever (fig. 25).[6]

Then there are the multilingual—simultaneously Latin-, Arabic-, Tatar-, and Italian-language—coins of Caffa (the Hellenist Theodosia in the Crimea). The Genoese mint that

23. Coin. Moscow. Silver denga. Circa 1389. Issued by Dimitri Donskoi. Petrov #14. Photo courtesy HCL.

24. Coin. Moscow. Silver denga. Issued by Ivan III (the Great) (1462–1505). Petrov 22. Photo courtesy HCL.

25. Coin. Denga. Circa 1425–46. Issued by Vasilii II Vasilievich (the Blind). Obverse: no legend, horseman riding, spearing serpent. Reverse: Pseudo-Arabic inscription. No Russian. Oreshnikov 529 (pl. ix, 382). Photo courtesy of Erik Schena.

operated there from the later fourteenth century to the mid-fifteenth century was in contact with the Golden Horde and then with the Ottomans. Many coins from Caffa had Tatar inscriptions on one side and "Banco di San Giorgio" on the other.[7]

For the region now called Ukraine, officials in Warsaw and Saint Petersburg issued, from 1832 to 1850, bilingual coins with the face value written in both Russian and Polish: from five kopecks (ten *groszy*) in silver to three rubles (twenty *zloty*) in gold.

Most such bilingual monies are crucial to the general history of comparative cultural iconography and semiotics. For the context of the United States, they raise the doubly semiotic issue concerning linguistic translation and monetary conversion. How should we translate one culture's already linguistic and monetary tokens, its semiotic system, in terms of another's? Americans in particular needed to be—and often were—astute at both monetary conversion and interlinguistic translation (figs. 26 and 27).

Consider here a typical "hard times" token from Louisiana. The Daquin Brothers, who were bakers in New Orleans, issued one such token (fig. 28). On the one hand, there is a linguistic translation: the phrase "bon pour un pain" translates as something like "good for one loaf of bread."[8] On the other hand, there is visual representation as potential exchange: the English inscription and the French inscription, taken together with the brass in which they both appear, transform the "engraved image" into a token exchangeable for either "*pain*" or "bread." The token is exchangeable for—it means—"a food article prepared by moistening, kneading, and baking meal or flour, generally with the addition of yeast or leaven."[9] Yet francophones and anglophones have different ideas about what that edible article should be. (We sometimes call these variable tastes national characteristics.) If the Daquin Brothers' token had a picture of the bread for which it was exchangeable, it would have been something like an interlinguistically useful monetary "pictograph." Automats present such in the flesh instead of representing them by words and pictures. A Frenchman would know automatically whether he was getting French bread or something that the English called bread.

One finds the same sort of bilingualism in various Louisiana banknotes. One example is the fifty-dollar bill printed in the 1820s and 1830s by the Louisiana Planters' Consolidated Association / L'Association Consolidée (1820s-1830s), which translates the term *dollars* as *piastres* (fig. 29).[10]

Problems of economic exchange and visual representation much concerned American producers of paper money and theorists of paper money, especially the multilingual thinkers like the German-American cartoonist Thomas Nast. Nast's now well-known cartoon *Milk Tickets for Babies in Place of Milk* (1876) serves as a case in point (fig. 30).[11] Nast includes a cartoon banknote that reads "This is a Howse and Lot by Act of the Architect." The word *Howse* is printed in the middle of a picture of the banknote, as if to say that there is adequation here between what is written and what is depicted and that the banknote as a whole requires both writing and picture.

Numismatic circumstances can involve witting or unwitting interlingual puns. Some of these are *mondegreens,* which involve hearing one word, or sound, as another.[12] A familiar example

TABLE OF DOLLARS and other COINS.

Number of Dollars, and Weight of Coins.	N.Hampshire, Massachusetts, Rhode Island, Connecticut, and Virginia.			New-York and N.Carolina			New Jersey, Pennsylvania, Maryland, and Delaware.			S.Carolina, and Georgia.		
Dols. 1	£.0	6	0	£.0	8	0	£.0	7	6	£.0	4	8
2	0	12	0	0	16	0	0	15	0	0	9	4
3	0	18	0	1	4	0	1	2	6	0	14	0
4	1	4	0	1	12	0	1	10	0	0	18	8
5	1	10	0	2	0	0	1	17	6	1	3	4
6	1	16	0	2	8	0	2	5	0	1	8	0
7	2	2	0	2	16	0	2	12	6	1	12	8
8	2	8	0	3	4	0	3	0	0	1	17	4
9	2	14	0	3	12	0	3	7	6	2	2	0
10	3	0	0	4	0	0	3	15	0	2	2	6
11	3	6	0	4	8	0	4	2	6	2	11	4
12	3	12	0	4	16	0	4	10	0	2	16	0
13	3	18	0	5	4	0	4	17	6	3	0	8
14	4	4	0	5	12	0	5	5	0	3	5	4
15	4	10	0	6	0	0	5	12	6	3	10	0
16	4	16	0	6	8	0	6	0	0	3	14	8
17	5	2	6	6	16	0	6	7	6	3	19	4
18	5	8	0	7	4	0	6	15	0	4	4	0
19	5	14	0	7	12	0	7	2	6	4	8	8
20	6	0	0	8	0	0	7	10	0	4	13	4
30	9	0	0	12	0	0	11	5	0	7	0	0
40	12	0	0	16	0	0	15	0	0	9	6	8
50	15	0	0	20	0	0	18	15	0	11	13	4
60	18	0	0	24	0	0	22	10	0	14	0	0
70	21	0	0	28	0	0	26	5	0	16	6	8
80	24	0	0	32	0	0	30	0	0	18	13	4
90	27	0	0	36	0	0	33	15	0	21	0	0
100	30	0	0	40	0	0	37	10	0	23	6	8
200	60	0	0	80	0	0	75	0	0	46	13	4
300	90	0	0	120	0	0	112	10	0	70	0	0
400	120	0	0	160	0	0	150	0	0	93	6	8
500	150	0	0	200	0	0	187	10	0	116	13	4
1000	300	0	0	400	0	0	375	0	0	233	6	8

	dwt.	gr.											
English Guinea,	5	6	£.1	8	0	£.1	17	0	£.1	15	0	£.1	1	9
French Guinea,	5	5	1	7	6	1	16	0	1	14	6	1	1	5
En. & F.Crown,	19	0	0	6	8	0	8	9	0	8	4	0	5	0
Half Johannes,	9	0	2	8	0	3	4	0	3	0	0	2	17	4
Pistole	4	5	1	2	0	1	8	0	1	7	0	0	17	6
Doubloon	17	0	4	8	0	5	16	0	5	12	0	3	10	0
Moidore	6	18	1	16	0	2	6	0	2	5	0	1	8	•

By a late regulation of the Assembly of S. Carolina, English Guineas must weigh 5 dwt. 7 gr. Pistole 4 dwt. 6 gr. and Moidores 6 dwt. 16 gr.

26. Table of Conversions, Dollars and Other Coins. Published in *The Philadelphia Directory, 1785.* Photo courtesy Library Company of Philadelphia.

	dwt.	gr.												
English Guinea,	5	6	£.1	8	0	£.1	17	0	£.1	15	0	£.1	1	9
French Guinea,	5	5	1	7	6	1	16	0	1	14	6	1	1	5
En. & F.Crown,	19	0	0	6	8	0	8	9	0	8	4	0	5	0
Half Johannes,	9	0	2	8	0	3	4	0	3	0	0	2	17	4
Pistole	4	5	1	2	0	1	8	0	1	7	0	0	17	6
Doubloon	17	0	4	8	0	5	16	0	5	12	0	3	10	0
Moidore	6	18	1	16	0	2	6	0	2	5	0	1	8	•

27. Detail, Table of Conversions, Dollars and Other Coins. 1785.

28. Bread-shop "bilingual" token.
New Orleans. 1835–42. Low 236. Rulau 115.

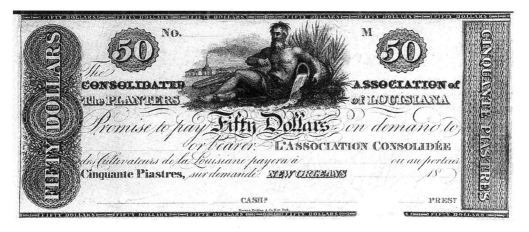

29. Banknote. Louisiana Planters' Consolidated Association / L'Association Consolidée.
Fifty dollars. 1820s–30s. CS.

30. Cartoon. Thomas Nast. *Milk Tickets for Babies in Place of Milk.* 1876. Wells. Photo courtesy HCL.

31. Banknote. What Cheer Bank, Providence, Rhode Island. Two dollars. 1863. American Banknote Company, New York. Durand p. 124.

32. Banknote. Agawam Bank, Springfield, Massachusetts. Five dollars. Not dated. *Agawam* means "where fish is cleaned" in the Algonquian language, Wampanoag tribe. Durand 33.

33. Banknote. Castine Bank, Castine, Massachusetts. Five dollars. Circa 1820. Paper Money, March/April 2005, whole no. 236. Collection of Q. David Bowers.

would be a young child's hearing the names of individual letters L M N O P in the "ABC Song"— sung to the tune of "Twinkle, Twinkle, Little Star"—as if they were a single word, *elemenopee,* with no apparent English-language meaning. Other interlingual puns are *false friends*: pairs of words in two languages that sound similar, or are spelled similarly, but differ in meaning.[13] Consider the false friend represented on banknotes issued to the What Cheer Bank in Providence, Rhode Island (fig. 31). The English-language phrase *What Cheer* probably derives from a Narragansett-English pidginization: "*Wha cheer netop.*"[14] A loose translation is, "Greetings, white man."[15] The Narragansett Indians supposedly said these words to the English-speaking Welsh missionary Roger Williams, whom they believed to be their true friend, when he arrived in Rhode Island.[16] Wrote Durfee in *What Cheer; or, Roger Williams in Banishment: A Poem* (1832):

"'Tis not the peäg [wampum]," said the sagamore [Indian King],
"Nor knives, nor guns, nor garments red as blood,
  That buy the lands I hold dominion o'er."[17]

In fact, much American paper money depicts the Indian braves greeting Williams—with "what cheer," on their part, as to the ultimate disposition of the land of the free and the home of the brave, we might well guess. Numismatic examples of "imaging of Indians" (as scholars sometimes call it) include banknotes from the Massachusetts towns of Agawam (fig. 32) and Castine (fig. 33); Ellsworth, Maine; and Florence, Nebraska (plate 14).[18] The American notion of paper money as pictograph bears on all such images.

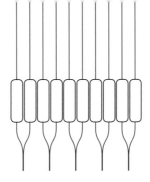

CHAPTER FOUR

Coins on Paper

HE RECEIVED THE PAPER VERY PEEVISHLY,
AND WAS ABOUT TO CRUMPLE IT,
APPARENTLY TO THROW IT IN THE FIRE,
WHEN A CASUAL GLANCE AT THE DESIGN
SEEMED SUDDENLY TO RIVET HIS ATTENTION.

——EDGAR ALLAN POE, *THE GOLD-BUG* (1843)

America is the birthplace of widely used paper money, and it has produced far more writing about paper money than any other country.[1] Much of that writing concerns questions of representation understood locally in terms of exchange. Bankers, for example, felt that depictions of houses and coins on paper convince people, whether illiterate or not, that the paper really does stand for—or is worth the same as—houses and coins. The fineness of reproduction or imitation, even as it makes counterfeiting more difficult, tends toward remaking the counterfeit into its own original.

Spanish and other coins were often depicted on paper monies (figs. 34, 35, and 36; plates 13, 15). Paper monies of an intercultural sort came to represent both American and Spanish specie at the same time. This is a moment of particular proud transition, as suggested in paper monies from Connecticut.

Many banknotes that represent coin also depict the Native Americans whose wampum the American colonists had once used as foreign legal tender. Banknotes from the Pocasset Bank in Massachusetts are good examples (fig. 37). The Pocasset tribe was led by a warrior queen, Weetamo. There is also a well-known Massachusetts note from the Wamsutta Bank (fig. 38), the

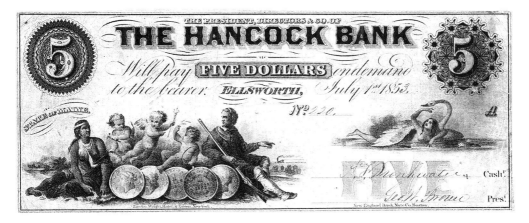

34. Banknote. Hancock Bank, Ellsworth, Maine. Five dollars. 1853.
Obsolete banknote series (1792–1866). The coins depicted are one-dollar
gold pieces. American Numismatic Association Money Museum.

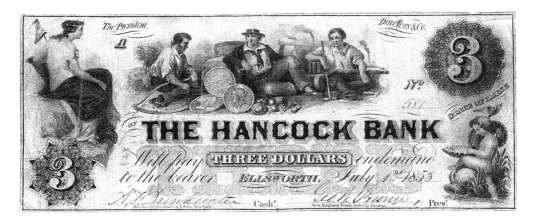

35. Banknote. Hancock Bank, Ellsworth, Maine. Three dollars. 1853.
Obsolete banknote series (1792–1866). American Numismatic Association Money Museum.

36. Banknote. Gold. Eureka, California. First National Gold Bank of San Francisco,
Charter 1741. Five dollars. 1870. Continental Bank Note Company of New York.
The central image is of U.S. gold coins current at the time, from one-dollar
to twenty-dollar pieces. American Numismatic Association Money Museum.

37. Banknote. Pocasset Bank, Fall River, Massachusetts. Two dollars. Not dated. Durand 95.

38. Banknote. Wamsutta Bank, Fall River, Massachusetts. Five dollars. 1889. Durand pp. 118–19.

39. Cartoon. Joke banknote. Humbug Glory Bank. Six cents. 1837.
An earlier version, slightly different, dates from 1834. Low 18A.

financial institution that got its name from the Wampanoag tribesperson who greeted Williams with those words "What Cheer." The chief Wamsutta was also known as Alexander, after the Macedonian conqueror, and his brother was called King Philip. Philip was an ally of Weetamo.

All such banknotes representing specie—and there are many—raise issues germane to numismatic and literary theory. Does paper represent specie? Is specie exchangeable for paper? Should coin always be nonfiduciary specie? Consider the bitter humor that informs one typical "joke banknote" of 1837 (fig. 39). This comic note helps to explain Poe's *Gold-Bug* in terms of the gold standard as literary humbug; its humor arises partly from a tradition of wampum misunderstood as pictographic scheme.[2]

Another cartoon from Thomas Nast, *A Shadow Is Not a Substance* (fig. 40), suggests a hardly more sophisticated apprehension about homegrown American paper currency and specie. In the foreground is an American eagle coin like the one represented on many American banknotes depicting Indians (fig. 41). Nast's cartoon pretends to interpret the economic issue of substantial value from the standpoint of the Greenbacks: coin is the "substance" and paper currency is its "shadow." Pondering Nast's *Milk Tickets for Babies in Place of Milk* (see fig. 30, p. 27), we might now want to ask a question about the cartoon banknote that depicts there a dollar sign, "$," by the act

40. Cartoon. Thomas Nast. *A Shadow Is Not a Substance*. 1876. Wells. Photo courtesy HCL.

41. Banknote. The Niantic Bank, Westerly, Rhode Island. One dollar. Not dated. Durand 80.

of Congress. Is money no more or less than the pictographic *shadow* of art? After all, the cartoon banknote that *depicts* a cow is—by act of the artists—a cow per se.

Nast's *A Shadow Is Not a Substance* obviously leaves out direct representation of the sun, which is so often appropriately depicted on coins as the ultimate source of wealth (fig. 42). The image of the sun as such, both numismatically and linguistically meaningful or meaningless, clearly recalls the doubloon nailed into the mast of the ship *Pequod* in Melville's *Moby-Dick*.[3] Nast's *Milk Tickets* focuses on conning—as in the cartoon banknote that reads "This is MILK by Act of Con," with its reference to Melville's *Confidence-Man*. Likewise, the cartoon spotlights "Congress"—as in the cartoon banknote that depicts a dollar sign, "$," and reads "This Is Money by the Act of Congress." More especially, even as the cartoon gives prominence to its inflated Humpty Dumpty rag doll, it makes the following quasi-Masonic claim: "THIS IS NOT ◇ R◇G B◇BY BUT ◇ REAL B◇BY BY ◇CT OF CONGRE." *Congress con*s people by means of *con*fidence. The *con*—and the jest—go back here to the common fear of being "suckered."

The all-American word *sucker* might seem here to have a partly monetary origin. As the joke note inscribed "Sucker Institution" suggests, a banknote with a picture of a suckerel (fig. 43)—a fish indigenous to America[4]—on it would make a sucker out of the bearer who believes the image can be cashed in for, or may as well be, the thing. Maybe this suckerel is not a suckerel.

René Magritte's painting appropriately called *La trahison des images* (The Treason of Images) (1929), with its celebrated drawing of a pipe and the inscription *Ceci n'est pas une pipe* (This is not a pipe), matches the devilishly jesting banknotes in Nast's *Milk Tickets*. One of these depicts a cow and is inscribed with the words "This is a Cow by the Act of the Artist"; another one depicts a house and is inscribed with the words "This is a Howse and Lot by the Act of the Architect." Both these jesting banknotes, and others included in *Milk Tickets*, recall the word

42. Coin. Ecuador. Four reales. 1842. Obverse: REPUBLICA DEL ECUADOR QUITO. ANS 1916.33.27. This image shows the sun, as depicted on this coin, casting the sort of shadow imagined in Nast's *A Shadow Is Not a Substance*.

43. Cartoon. Joke banknote. Sucker Institution, Guard Wall, Pennsylvania. Ten cents. 1837. Low 25.

Act (*Tat*) by which, the German-American Nast reminds us, Faust translated the biblical Word (*Wort*) of the Bible in Goethe's *Faust Part One* (1808). Faust's active translation is prelude to the con artist's Mephisophelean creation of paper money in Goethe's *Faust Part Two* (1832). Goethe has in mind John Law's paper money experiment in the 1720s, when French *assignats*, or paper monies, were "assigned" to the real estate of the New World. Nast has in mind the way in which a purportedly specifically American monetary inscription on a banknote depicting the dollar sign, "$," claims to be money itself: "I am Money by Act of Congress." *In Hoc Signo.*

In Melville's too-trusting America, it surely seems as if "there's a sucker born every minute," as the famous American confidence trickster Joseph Bessimer used to say. (The same saying is also attributed to the circus master P. T. Barnum.)[5] It is a sign of how far gone the Indian languages are, these days, that almost no one who has seen the joke banknote note from Sucker Institution has understood its obviously multilingual pun. William Wood remarks in his "Small Nomenclator of the Indian Language" (1634)—which was used as a school text in the New England colonies in the seventeenth century[6]—that *suckis suacke* means "clam." Roger Williams notes in his *Key into the Language of America* (1643) that *suckau* is abbreviated Indian lingo for wampum of a kind: "Their white [money] they call *Wompam* (which signifies white), their black *suckauhock* (*sucki* signifying blacke)."[7] Students of America, its culture of trust and distrust, should follow Roger Williams's advice to learn something of the first American languages; their ghostly lexis and syntax yet abide with us.[8]

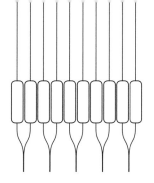

CHAPTER FIVE

What Is Wampum?

KAWKENOG WAMPOMPEAGE—LET ME SEE MONEY.

—WILLIAM WOOD, "A SMALL NOMENCLATOR
OF THE INDIAN LANGUAGE" (1634)

———

BUT THEIR MOST MYSTERIOUS FABRIC WAS WAMPUM.
THIS WAS AT ONCE THEIR CURRENCY,
THEIR ORNAMENT, THEIR PEN, INK,
AND PARCHMENT; AND ITS USE
WAS BY NO MEANS CONFINED TO
TRIBES OF THE IROQUOIS STOCK.

—FRANCIS PARKMAN,
THE JESUITS IN NORTH AMERICA (1867)

The English term *wampum* means those generally tubular beads made from clam or conch shell (see plates 2–7). Europeans often used these shells for what they call "mercenary transactions." So it is no wonder that Linnaeus in 1758 gave the name *Mercenaria mercenaria* to quahogs, cherrystones, and periwinkles. Woodward wrote in *A Manual of the Mollusca* in 1856, "The North American Indians used to make coinage (wampum) of the sea-worn fragments of *Venus mercenaria*."[1] In this way too, both the Swedish taxonomist and the British conchologist decided what is mercenary and what coinage. However, such economic ethno-conchology, as it is called, has its limits when attention to the material of the conch drives out consideration of its role in the symbolic "ethics" of exchange.[2]

The First Peoples around Chabougamau, Québec—where I grew up—had many terms for wampum.[3] Sébastien Rasles, in his great dictionary of the Abnaki language (1691), says that *wampum* itself derives from the Algonquian *wampi,* meaning "white," and *umpe,* meaning "string."[4] A near synonym is *peag,* and sometimes, Rasles says, the "two words [*wampi* and *umpe*] were combined" (as some would have it) into *wampumpeag.* (The division of *wampum* from *peag* seems to be what the *OED* calls "a false analysis due to Europeans" who did not understand that the full term actually was *wampampiak* or *wampampial*.) Other such terms in Native American languages would include *onehkohra* (Mohawk) and *roanoke*.[5] Various Iroquoian terms have been the subject of special studies, for example, *8ânbobi* (Abnaki), *mikis* (Algonquin), and *megis* (Ojibwa).[6]

The European settlers, traders, and conquerors had various words for *wampum*. The Dutch preferred *zeewan[t]* and *sewan[t]*.[7] The French had *gaionne*.[8] In his description of wampum in *Voyages* (1534–36), Jacques Cartier—who reports on Hochelaga (later Montréal)—uses the term *esurgny*: "La plus precieuse chose qu'ilz ayent en ce monde, est Esurgny" ("That which they hold in highest estimation among all their possessions, is a substance which they call *esurgny* or *cornibotz*").[9] Hale, citing Bruyas's *Radices verborum Iroquæorum* (1863), interprets *esurgny* as the Iroquois *ionni*.[10] French writers debate whether to use *porcelaine* (associated with the *Cypraea porcellana,* or cowry shell, and also with the *Cypraea moneta*) or *wampum* (preferred by most French Jesuits) (fig. 44). English-language translators of the royal geographer Samuel de Champlain's *Des Sauvages* (1604) and his two *Voyages* (1613, 1619) argue similarly about whether to use *porcelain* or *wampum*.[11] In fact, *porcelaine* fell out of favor as soon as the French traders began to make "counterfeit" wampum from semitranslucent glazed earthenware (porcelain).[12]

The profusion of terms for wampum is not surprising. The objects we call wampum serve as common media in various languages of the New World. Moreover, shells play an important economic role in exchange in many more economic systems. Jevons, in his *Money and the Mechanism of Exchange* (1875), makes an argument about "cowry shells, which under one name

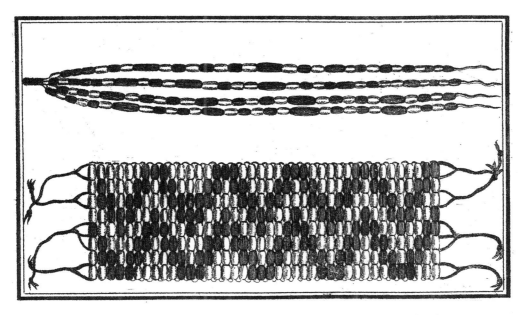

44. Wampum. Iroquois. 1722. From M. de Bacqueville de la Potherie, *Histoire de l'Amérique septentrionale,* **4 vols. (Paris: Jean-Luc Nion et François Didot, 1722), 1:334.**
By permission of the Houghton Library, Harvard University.

or another—*chamgos, zimbis, bourges, porcelanes,* &c.—have long been used" (italics mine).[13] In the New World itself, wampum mediated among various terms for shells used as a medium of exchange and representation. However, wampum was not only part of a linguistic lingua franca. Wampum also suggested or actually became a commercial lingua franca, or international trading medium, not only for the various Indian groups, but also, intermittently, among the various European ones. For example, there was, as Balmer suggests, sometimes "a perfect babel of confusion" among the Europeans.[14] (Balmer was writing about Dutch and English speakers in the colonies of New York and New Jersey, that is, in New Amsterdam and New Netherland.) Wampum was often the sole medium that allowed for communication and for providing acceptable, even legal, tender.

In his *Description of New Netherland* (1655), van der Donck reports the early use of wampum as legal tender:

> That there should be no miserly desire for the costly metals among the natives, few will believe; still it is true, the use of gold and silver or any metallic coin is unknown among them. The currency which they use in their places to which they resort is called *wampum,* the making and preparing of which is free to all persons. . . . This is the only article of moneyed medium among the natives, with which any traffic can be driven; and it is also common with us in purchasing necessaries and carrying on our trade; many thousand strings are exchanged every year for peltries near the sea shores where the wampum is only made, and where the peltries are brought for sale. Among the Netherlanders gold and silver begin to increase and are current, but still the amount differs much from that of the Netherlands.[15]

45. **Crest insignium. Province of New Brunswick, Canada. The galley represents the ships that brought the Loyalists to the province. The motto is usually translated as "Hope Restored." Archives and Research Library, New Brunswick Museum, Saint John, New Brunswick.**

The same reliance on wampum obtained for the New England traders. (Exceptionally, wampum was not adopted as legal tender by New France, which famously remained at a precapitalist stage even as it adopted playing-card money on the model of wampum.)[16]

Put otherwise: wampum was the monetary lingua franca, a sort of economist's trade language, like Chinook or Choctaw. In a description of a conference held with the Indians in Hochelaga (Montreal) in 1756, one reporter writes, "These [wampum] belts and strings of wampum are the universal agent among Indians."[17] Wampum was what Karl Marx calls the essential monetary *and* linguistic aspect of the "language of commodities."[18] Gilbert Parker accordingly writes in his *Mrs. Falchion: A Novel* (1893) that wampum was a lingua franca for "tribes and peoples" who were otherwise linguistically disparate.[19] In fact, it is an image of wampum that binds together the two official language groups of New Brunswick. On that Canadian province's official crest appears both the British shield ("Union Jack"), carried by the stag on the left, and the French shield ("Fleur de Lys"), carried by the stag on the right, with both stags happily wearing the same kind of *wampum* collar (fig. 45).[20]

Wampum as "pledge" often serves this sort of interlinguistic function. John Richardson, in his poem *Tecumseh, or, The Warrior of the West* (1828), writes:

> The wampum pledge is pass'd from hand to hand
> As in due order moves each warrior chief,
> To say the feelings of his sep'rate band
> And in strange tongues, yet energetic, brief.[21]

In *On Some Words Derived from Languages of North American Indians* (1872), J. Hammond Trumbull notes the complex intertribal traditions here: "The names which the English and Dutch gave to the bead-work and shell-money of the Indians—*wampum, peag, seewand* or *sewan,* etc.—were all of Algonkin derivation, yet none of them was used by the Indians in their own language in the sense in which it was understood by the colonists."[22] The American colonists saw something in wampum that the Indians did not see, and vice versa.

The French writer Bacqueville de la Potherie argues in his *History of North America* (1722) that Iroquois wampum is a definite sort of *écriture* (scripture). Wampum he says, "is their writing for making peace treaties, for diplomacy, for expressing their thoughts, for settling disputes, for condemnation or for absolution; it serves as an ornament for young warriors going to battle, who make it into bracelets and belts which they place on their white shirts."[23] The linguistic and monetary exchange systems that the Europeans in America were using and observing were themselves changing rapidly thanks to the various kinds of encounters and interactions—and especially treaties—that inform the economic and cultural history of North America.

The European- and Colonial-style wampum belts include the Penn Belt (fig. 46), which was supposedly delivered by the Leni-Lenape sachems to William Penn at the signing of the treaty under the elm tree at Shackamaxon in 1682; the Washington Covenant Belt (fig. 47), a

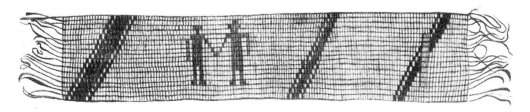

46. Penn Belt. 1682. Beauchamp 173.

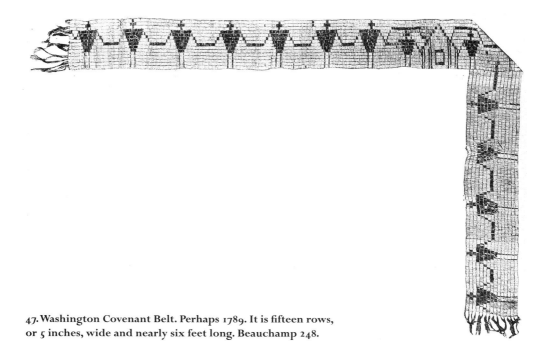

47. Washington Covenant Belt. Perhaps 1789. It is fifteen rows, or 5 inches, wide and nearly six feet long. Beauchamp 248.

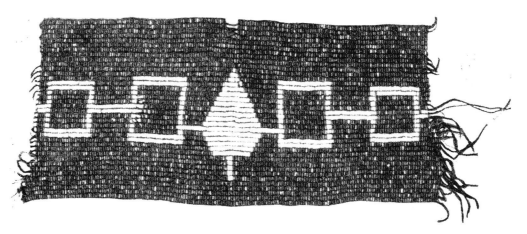

48. League Belt. Date not known (before 1878). Beauchamp 252.

49. Tribal belt. Probably after 1712. Beauchamp 277.

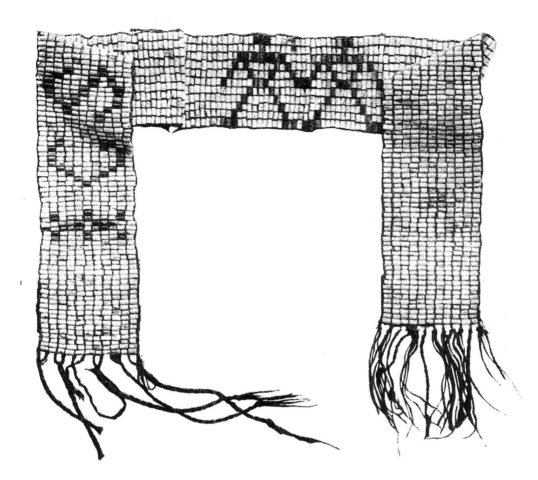

50. Simcoe Belt. Probably 1790s. Beauchamp 269.

record of the treaty with General Washington; the League Belt (fig. 48), sometimes called the
Hiawatha Belt, reputedly a record of the formation of the Haudenosaunee Confederacy; the
Oneida Tribal Belt (fig. 49), whose six diamonds probably represent also the Tuscaroras; and the
Simcoe Belt (fig. 50), bearing the letters I G S, the initials of John [Iohannes] Graves Simcoe,
Governor General of Upper Canada, who formed an alliance with the Indians.[24]

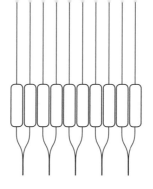

CHAPTER SIX

Indian Giving and Willie Wampum

TAKE YOU THE WAMPUM, AND OUR LOVE.

——JAMES FENIMORE COOPER,
THE LAST OF THE MOHICANS (1826)

Native Americans used wampum for a variety of purposes oftentimes kept apparently discrete in European cultures: ransom (fig. 51), bride-wealth, compensation for death, treaties, trade, cash money, commodity, and so forth. Harriet Maxwell Converse, for example, said that the ransom belt "could save a life if presented by the youngest unmarried female in the family."[1] The distinction between "Native American" and "European" is so commonplace and fraught with intellectual troubles, however, as to make exchange difficult to understand on both sides. Each side has a predilection to rely too much on the dichotomy between "their" monetary systems and "ours"—the primitive versus the modern, say, or the simple versus the complex.[2]

There is, of course, a dichotomy between the commercial and noncommercial realms in much European Christianity. Various doctrines put down purportedly non-Christian practices in exchanging goods. Consider, for example the derogatory American English–language phrase *Indian giver*. This term has had two interrelated pseudo-secular meanings.

The first meaning of *Indian giver* involves giving a gift and then demanding its return. That has been the usual meaning since the early twentieth century. This first meaning—"one who

51. Ransom belt. Date unknown. Beauchamp 247.

takes back a gift"——expresses less the European Americans' mistaking Indian loans for free gifts, which is how some scholars see it.[3] It more expresses the European Americans' projecting, unto various Indian groups, the practices that they did not want to recognize in themselves: the European Americans themselves famously cheated the Indians by giving their word in treaties (wampum) and then withdrawing it. William Wood, in his "Small Nomenclator of the Indian Language" (1634), thus misinterprets the Massachusetts Indians' *kettotanese* as simply "Lend me money" and *commouton kean* as plainly "You steal."[4] Mark Twain picks up the theme in his *Life on the Mississippi* (1883): "Who can it be that has dared to steal my wampum?"[5]

The second meaning of *Indian giver* involves a person who gives a gift while expecting to receive a counter-gift of equal worth. That was its usual meaning since the eighteenth century.[6] Massachusetts Lieutenant-Governor and Chief-Justice Thomas Hutchinson writes in his *History of the Colony of Massachusetts-Bay* (1765), "An Indian gift is a proverbial expression, signifying a present for which an equivalent return is expected."[7] Hutchinson was writing some fifteen years after King George's War, when he had "redeemed," or "made good on," paper money issued by Massachusetts to its war veterans. The situation he faced then recalled paper money experiments in the 1690s and in the 1740s.[8]

Both meanings of *Indian giver* have obvious reference to finance and commerce. However, the second meaning of the phrase—one who expects a counter-gift—expresses a certain misapprehension, either of Native American ways of trade, barter, and exchange or of European ways (which those who call other people Indian givers apparently suppose to involve giving gifts without expectation of counter-gifts) or of both Indian and European ways. For many peoples, after all, commerce and gift-giving are parts of a continuum. For givers and takers of this sort, there is a relatively open acknowledgment of the polar opposition between two types of transactions. The first type involves the recipient's returning to the giver the actual item given (the first meaning of *Indian giving*)—as if such an ideal return were not always partly compromised due to issues of wear and tear and lost use. The second type of transaction involves the recipient's giving to the giver an item of equal worth to the gift item that was given (the second meaning of *Indian giving*). For Christians as such, however, there is often, if not usually, no open acknowledgment. To be sure, European Christian ways of thinking about this matter do differ greatly among Protestant-English and Protestant-Dutch groups as well as among Catholic-Spanish and Catholic-French ones, especially in the New World. But all these groups divide gift-giving and commerce along a defining real/ideal polar dialectic. On the one hand, there is the supposedly *mercenary/commercial* (secular) aspect of life. That aspect is often associated explicitly with a money devil, usually linked with such "humanoid" groups as Jews (in the Old World) and Indians (in the New World).[9] On the other hand, there is the supposedly *merciful/anticommercial* (religious) part of life.[10] Christ throws the changers of money (or real *merces*) out of the temple and offers the people *mercy* (or ideal grace or love) instead.

Is there really such a thing as a freely given gift? The question, once posed in this way, is already a matter of theology.[11] Likewise, whether a counter-gift ever amounts to the actual first gift is a quandary apparently solved, on a pseudo-secular level, by the idea of specifically Christian resurrection whereby life itself is redeemed. So much is certain: Indian giving—the way that Indians were exchanging goods and understanding the meaning of that exchange—beneficially affected the conquerors of the land and its people in the monetary sphere, as we shall see. At the same time, however, Indian ways challenged those conquerors uncomfortably on the religious plane in such a way that they often wanted, almost to the point of pathology, the Indians' conversion to English Christianity. American pseudo-secular holidays such as Thanksgiving seem almost to balance the good Indians' "giving generously" against the bad Indians' "Indian giving"—a projection of the settler's eventual lack of gratitude.

"Language has always been the companion of empire," as Tzvetan Todorov writes in *The Conquest of America*.[12] But for American Christians in the New World, it is also often religion that must go together with language. "And they spoke to me in the Christian language" is how Omar ibn Said put it in the 1830s. (Omar was a Fula- or Arabic-speaking African Muslim enslaved in the United States in the 1830s.)[13]

Generally speaking, too little attention is paid to the socio- and psychopathologies of the diverse Christian Europeans' variously national systems of monetary exchange in the New World, whether those Europeans spoke English, Dutch, Spanish, or French, and likewise whether they were Protestant or Catholic. We might subsume the study of this pathology under a heading such as *fetish,* a term that originates with "civilized" Portuguese descriptions of "savage" peoples in East Africa and was extended by the Frenchman Charles de Brosses (1760), the German Karl Marx, and the Austrian Sigmund Freud.[14]

The link between European-style totemism and American mascotry is often apparent in modern American practices. In this context, a *mascot* is "a thing used to symbolize a particular event or organization."[15] *Mascotry* as such is associated with *totemism* in the anthropological and literary tradition that includes the work of Frazer and Claude Lévi-Strauss.[16] For our purposes, the relevant example of mascotry comes from the American sports world of football, since it has often made use of Indian mascots.

Stanford Indians was the name of Stanford University's football team when I arrived there as an undergraduate transfer student from Québec in 1965. The Stanford Indians had an Indian mascot who provided Stanford's students with a large-nosed theatrical figure dancing on cue for the spectators and providing administrators with fun and funds. (The mascot had to wear a papier-mâché head that was four feet high.) In 1965 there was, judging from the records, only *one* actual Indian student enrolled at the college.

During the same period, Marquette University also had a football team with an Indian mascot. (Other American universities too had Indian mascots.)[17] The name of Marquette's mascot was Willie Wampum.[18] What sort of name was that? Why did so many people like the name so much? The term *willie* has two relevant meanings. First, *willie* refers to certain animals. Among these animals are willocks (guillemots) and willy wagtails (water wagtails), which are kinds of birds, and willy goats (billy goats). Second, *willie* is "a slang name for a child's penis."[19] Gregor Ian Smith's children's book *The Story of Willie Wampum: A Red Indian* (1955) suggests a formative influence on the undergraduate student body of the time.[20] (My first Stanford roommates knew the book from their childhoods.)

In any case, college students and alumni simply adored their mascot Willie Wampum. Many postwar movies also treated Indian exchange systems—both linguistic and monetary—as childish. In Howard Hawks's *Monkey Business* (1952), for example, Cary Grant plays a scientist, Barnaby Fulton, who is transformed into a child who runs with playmates chanting, "Me wantum wampum, ugh, ugh, ugh."[21] In Anglo-American culture, *ugh* is often an interjection expressive of disgust, at least when it is not comedic, as in the novelist Thackeray's sometimes multilingual novel *The Virginians: A Tale of the Last Century* (1859): "'*Ah, canaille, tu veux du sang? Prends!*' said Florac, with a curse; and the next moment, and with an *ugh,* the Indian fell over my chest dead, with Florac's sword through his body." Laurence Oliphant—superintendent of Indian affairs in Canada—wrote in his *Episodes in a Life of Adventure* (1887), "My address was frequently interrupted by what [James Fenimore] Cooper calls 'expressive ughs.'"[22] In fact, Cooper's Indian characters often use the term *hugh*. In his *Last of the Mohicans*—written about the French and Indian War—*hugh* has an assentant meaning much like the English-Choctaw term *okay*.[23]

America's long-standing cultural need to parody Indian ways of speaking by way of mockery ("ugh, ugh, ugh") often matches its polar opposite want to think of certain Indian ways of speaking as exemplary. On the one hand, such voice men as Mel Blanc imitated the supposedly barbarian and stammering sound of Indian speakers in popular radio programs like *The Jack Benny Show*.[24] (Blanc is best known for imitating such speech-impeded talking animals in the movies as Warner Brothers' Porky Pig.) On the other hand, there is the American myth, based on faulty scholarship, that unlike the members of any other group, no Indians stutter—which is what Wendell Johnson, once the best known of American speech therapists, argued.[25]

Did students and university alumni at Marquette and Stanford universities have some nervous apprehension—"the willies"—about wampum and Indians? Should their good-humored academic mascotism, with its overt suggestions of infantile sexuality, be linked willy-nilly with conceptual animalization of Indians or with Stanford's near-total totemic exclusion of them from the student body? Let us not make a mountain out of this molehill or convert ideally kind gifts into actual hoaxes. Certain Europeans have long criticized the mascotry at work within Christian sects themselves. The London-based Religious Tract Society, for example, put forth in 1923 that "there is a worse aspect of mascotry than mere folly . . . for mascotry is, in its essence, simply idolatry."[26]

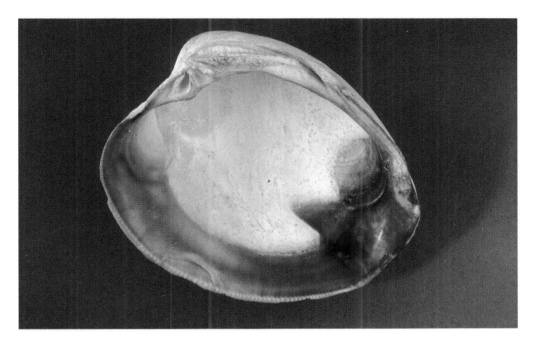

Plate 1. Quahog shell for making wampum. Nineteenth century.
Peabody Museum of Archaeology and Ethnology, Harvard University.

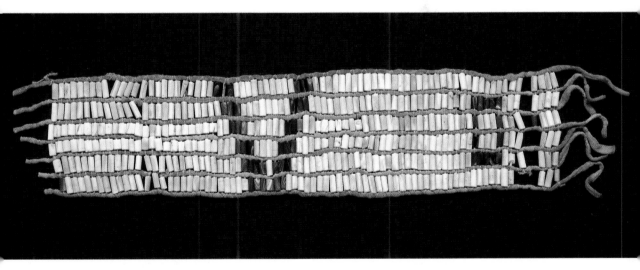

Plate 2. Wampum belt. Huron-Wendat. Shells and leather. Photo courtesy Musée de la civilisation,
Archives du Séminaire de Québec. Idra Labrie, Perspective, photographer. No. 96-1080.

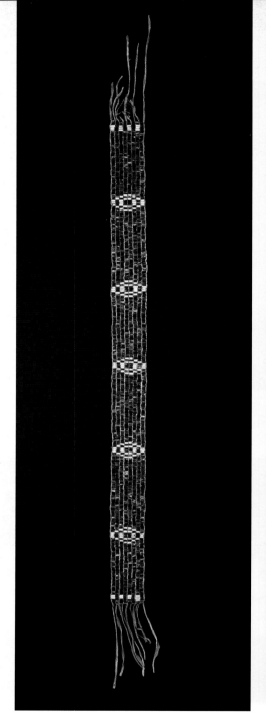

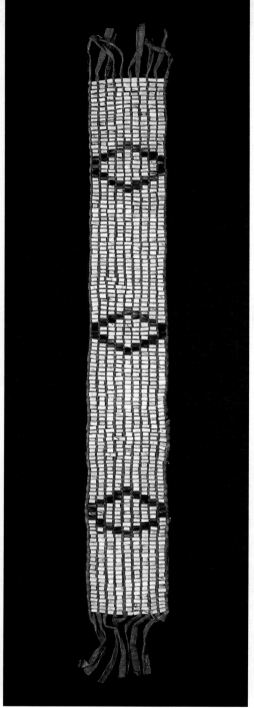

Plate 3. Wampum. Huron-Wendat. Shells and leather. Collection Cyrille Tessier. Photo courtesy Musée de la civilisation, Archives du Séminaire de Québec. Idra Labrie, Perspective, photographer. No. 1992.1288.

Plate 4. Wampum. Huron-Wendat. Shells and leather. Collection Cyrille Tessier. Photo courtesy Musée de la civilisation, Archives du Séminaire de Québec. Idra Labrie, Perspective, photographer. No. 1992.1289.

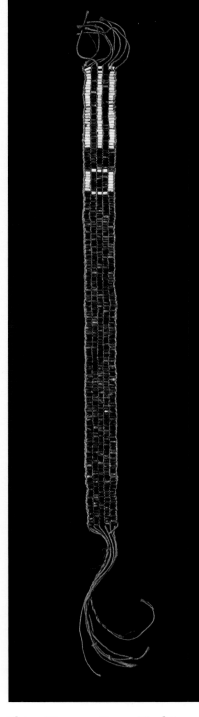

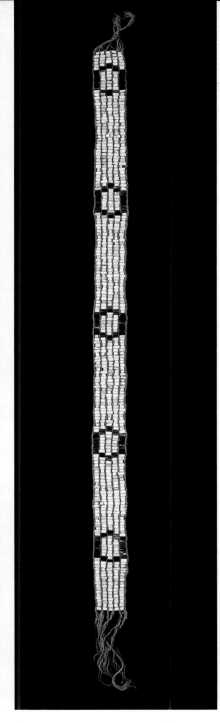

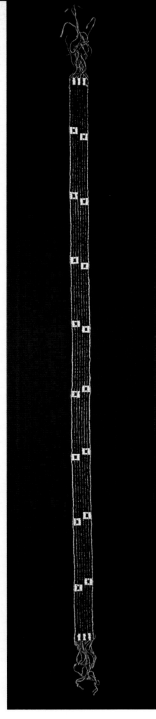

Plate 5. Wampum. Huron-Wendat. Shells, leather, and plant fiber. Collection Cyrille Tessier. Photo courtesy Musée de la civilisation, Archives du Séminaire de Québec. Idra Labrie, Perspective, photographer. No. 1992.1290.

Plate 6. Wampum. Huron-Wendat. Shells and plant fiber. Collection Cyrille Tessier. Photo courtesy Musée de la civilisation, Archives du Séminaire de Québec. Idra Labrie, Perspective, photographer. No. 1992.1291.

Plate 7. Wampum belt. Huron-Wendat. Glass and leather. Collection Cyrille Tessier. Photo courtesy Musée de la civilisation, Archives du Séminaire de Québec. Idra Labrie, Perspective, photographer. No. 1992.1292.

Plate 8. Engraving. Charles Grignion. After Benjamin West, *The Indians Giving a Talk to Colonel Bouquet* (1766). West depicted the October 1764 meeting between British representatives led by Colonel Henry Bouquet and a delegation of Shawnee, Delaware, and Ohio Indians. HCL.

Plate 9. Cartoon. W. Humphreys. *The Tea-Tax-Tempest or Old Time with His Magic Lantern.* London. March 12, 1783. Photo courtesy The Lilly Library, Indiana University, Bloomington.

Plate 10. Jan Verelst. Portrait of Tee Yee Neen Ho Ga Row ("Hendrick"). London, 1710. Oil on canvas. Tee Yee Neen Ho Ga Row was dubbed Emperor of the Six Nations after meeting with Queen Anne. Library and Archives Canada, C-092414.

Plate 11. One-cent coin. Commonwealth of Massachusetts. 1787 and/or 1788. First American coin with the cent denomination. ANS 1911.85.4.

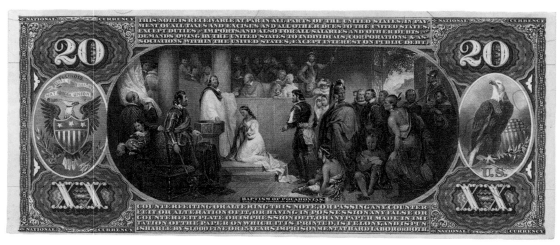

Plate 12. National Bank Note. First Charter Period. Twenty dollars. 1863–75. Shows Pocahontas being baptized in 1613. American Numismatic Association Money Museum.

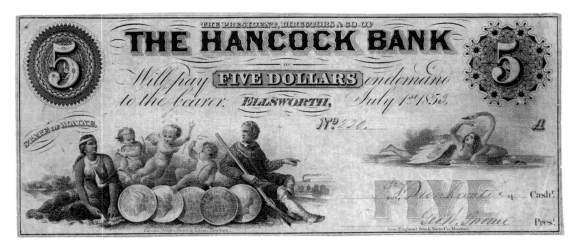

Plate 13. Banknote. Hancock Bank. Ellsworth, Maine. Five dollars. 1853. CS.

Plate 14. Banknote. Bank of Florence.
Florence, Nebraska. One dollar. 1858.
Smithsonian Institution, Washington, D.C.

Plate 15. Banknote. Gold. First National Gold Bank of San Francisco.
Eureka, California. Five dollars. 1870. CS.

Plate 16. Coin. Salt Lake City, Utah.
Gold. Five dollars. 1860. CS.

Plate 17. *Old King George; or, The Last Laugh.* **Painting by Otis Kaye. 1930s. CS.**

Plate 18. *Battle of Little Big Horn.* **Painting by Otis Kaye. 1951. CS.**

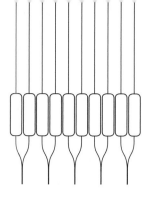

CHAPTER SEVEN

Money Writing

A GOOD SPEAKER WILL BE ABLE TO POINT OUT THE
EXACT PLACE ON A [WAMPUM] BELT WHICH IS TO
ANSWER TO EACH PARTICULAR SENTENCE, THE SAME
AS WE CAN POINT OUT A PASSAGE IN A BOOK.

——JOHN HECKEWELDER,
ACCOUNT OF THE INDIAN NATIONS (1819)

It has been common practice for a century or more to lump together many indigenous groups living in what is now the United States and then call them all "Indian," as if all were one group. From this point of view, it hardly matters which term one uses: *Aboriginal, Autochthon, American Indian, Amerindian, Indian, Indigen, Injun, Native, Native American, North American Indian, Original Inhabitant, Red Indian, Red Man, Redskin,* and *Savage* are all one, and plural names like *First Nations* and *First Peoples* work the same. Every one of these terms tends, each in its own more-or-less politically acceptable or unacceptable way, toward homogenizing a large collection of tribes or nations into one grouping. (Compare such catchall, culture-shaping—or, if you prefer, culture-misshaping—terms as contemporary anglophone America's *Hispanic* and *Asian American*.)[1] This tendency to group together different nationalities is not only a European's intellectual and political problem but also an Indian's dilemma. Georges Sioui, who is of Wyandot-Huron descent, calls for an "autohistoire amérindienne"—presumably a history of Indians written by Indians, but that would require an almost superhuman knowledge of the various tribal languages and dialects at issue.[2] The problem is all the more intense when it comes to wampum. After all, interpretations of *wampum* come from people of nationally and linguistically different cultures and languages who peremptorily amalgamate the "exchange" traditions of many different kinship and dialect groups as if all Indian groups were the same. For example, some students of wampum do not even try to figure what it means that, in most specifically Algonquian languages, the term for wampum is generally a nonanimate, or inanimate, noun, while at the same time, they insist that wampum is a "living symbol" or even an "animated noun."[3]

Algonquian languages have animate and nonanimate nouns in much the same way that French has male and female nouns. The various words for wampum are usually inanimate. (The view that *wampum* is always animate is usually incorrect.)[4] The fiduciary difference between coin and paper money—and, in certain circumstances, that between ingot and coin—informs the always crucial distinction in Algonquian languages between animate and inanimate. As the linguist Conor Quinn observes about the Algonquian Penobscot language, one term, *awíhkhikan*, is *animate* when it means "inscription of any sort; pictograph; glyph, hieroglyphic," but the same term is *inanimate* when it refers to "an item with glyphs on it," such as a book or coin. In Penobscot, "*glyphic* items are animate not for having glyphs impressed or written on them, but for actually being glyphs themselves." According to Quinn, this difference between inscription and inscribed thing helps to explain "why *money* is not inherently animate; [money] is not a glyphic item itself. Contrast animate *nəkət kiso* [silver dollar] with inanimate *nəkətakísəwiyə* [dollar bill]; a dollar bill is a banknote, more like a book or piece of writing than like the glyphs printed on it." Quinn's own analysis puzzles him: "both coinage and banknotes have this feature; why are only coins animate?"[5] The quandary dissipates, however, when one sees what coin and ingot share in common.

Ingots are the sunlike, disk- or coin-shaped objects (*anəskaman*) on the chest of the Native American woman Molly Molasses, as depicted in an old photograph (fig. 52), that suggest to Quinn the problematically animate and inanimate status of money and its glyphic and epigraphic aspect.[6] Also known as Mary Balassee Nicola, Molly Molasses is a well-known figure in American letters. Henry David Thoreau writes about her in "The Allegash and East Branch" (1864).[7] Beauchamp includes a photograph of her wampum marriage belt (fig. 53) in the collection he published in Québec in 1901.[8] Quinn wondered how the remarkable disks (fig. 54) were used by the Penobscot, and Fannie Hardy Eckstorm commented on their creation, noting that "our Indians did no silver work themselves; they never 'cold hammered' silver; but the silver brooches replaced aboriginal ornaments of a similar design, made from beads, quills or native substances."[9] Several earlier writers, including Frank Speck (1919), also raised the issue of the disks' use.[10] Some modern anthropologists say that these objects are "jewelry" and others say that they are "monetary objects." Neither side, however, wants to consider how jewelry serves as money and money serves as jewelry. The brilliant Abnaki grammarian Joseph Laurent, a tribal chief who published his work in Québec, comes closer to the mark when, in his *Abenakis and English Dialogues* (1884), he treats *môni* ("dollar") as inanimate and *sansak* ("cents") as animate.[11] So too does the eighteenth-century historian Beverley, who calls these disks *runtees* in his *History of Virginia* (1722).[12]

The process and consequences of European scholars' ignoring such crucial nuances as the animate/inanimate dialectic in the various Indian languages are everywhere evident: most scholars overlook the actual sense of works available in bilingual format, such as *Wapapi Ako-nutomakonol* (1893).[13] With few exceptions, American universities, even those that offer affirmative action programs for persons of Native American descent, are nowadays more or less willing purveyors of non-anglophone American illiteracy and eventual linguicide of the Native American languages.

Were the anglophone Americans of the twentieth century really so traumatized by the genocide of Indians that they could not bring themselves to study the Indian languages? Already by the 1830s, Americans counted themselves clear victors over the land. They were now living

52. **Mary Balassee Nicola, known as Molly Molasses. Old Town, Maine. Photograph and monochrome, March 16, 1865, by Isabel Eaton, held at the Bangor Historical Society. Eckstorm 190, 192, insert between pages 178 and 179.**

53. **Penobscot marriage belt said to have belonged to Molly Molasses. Date unknown. Beauchamp 279.**

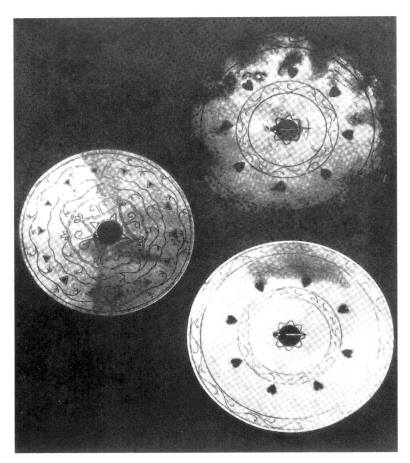

54. Penobscot and possibly Passamaquoddy disks. Diameters: 6″ to 7″.
Maine Historical Society. Bequest of Mary Purinton Putnam.
Eckstorm, insert between pages 178 and 179.

comfortably in a ghost land left behind by one-time friends and foes. Trauma does allow for
a forgetting and eventual reshaping of the past; in fact, trauma may even require them, for a
while, as a sort of heuristically useful device along the road to cure or knowledge. Yet scholars
in America were actively reduplicating, at the ideal level of monetary and numismatic historiography, the real annihilation of Indian peoples. American universities' ongoing inattention to
indigenous languages and cultures ideally recapitulates that same real annihilation. The distress-
ing consequence here is the continuing process and powerful procedures of American-languages
linguicide among both Indians and non-Indians.

A proper Yankee professor should complain about this reduplication. After all, Harvard,
with its famed "Indian College," reliably teaches hardly a single Native North American language. Ironically, Harvard's huge treasure-house still holds vast quantities of wampum, or its

equivalent, from when wampum was legal tender in Massachusetts, a time when writers such as Thomas Lechford in his *Plain Dealing* (1641) complained that Puritan coreligionists were contributing imperfect wampum at the church collection.[14] Many of the first gifts to Harvard were donated in that foreign yet native currency. Writes George Bancroft in his *History of the United States* (1876), "The farmers and seamen of Massachusetts nourished its college with coin and strings of wampum."[15] Even in New Netherland, seventeenth-century residents knew the official Indian wampum, Dutch styver, and English pence "conversion rates" for the ferriage routes between Brooklyn and Manhattan.[16]

For Europeans, one consequence of the discovery of America was the certain knowledge that there were many more languages—and dialects—in the world than they had imagined.[17] This knowledge triggered a new science of linguistics that came to fruition in the nineteenth century around the time that most of the languages themselves were rapidly disappearing. In the shorter term, linguistic encounters between Indians and Europeans involved both sides in more practical experiments in communication: pantomime (or silent trade) and sign language, for example.[18] Communication was not always aimed at amassing dominant power. ("Among the preconditions for establishing regimes of colonial power was, must have been, communication with the colonized," writes Fabian. He is surely correct to add that this goes "beyond the [trivial] fact of verbal exchange" and includes such communication as wampum. But communication as such is not always aimed at establishing colonial power.)[19] There were variously organized "exchange programs" for educating linguistic and economic go-betweens or mediators: intermarriage was often encouraged among francophone Catholics, and European-American children of all language groups were sometimes placed out in the homes of Native Americans.[20] The eighteenth-century *métis*, or "half-breed," John Montour was one such: he "memorized the speech on wampum belts" and "translated, but did not speak."[21] None of this solved essential political problems in linguistic communication: the possibility of betrayal by the translator, for example, all the more especially so when speakers would slyly speak a patois because their own language was sacred in such a way that it required concealment from others.[22]

Pidgin languages sometimes arise where there is rough equality among the groups interacting, as among the Basques and Mi'kmaqs in the Gulf of the Saint Lawrence.[23] To facilitate trade, a number of trade languages known as pidgins developed: languages with limited vocabulary and a simplified grammar that enabled people with different native languages to communicate. Eskimo trade jargon, Mednyj Aleut, Chinook Jargon, Michif, and Choctaw Mobilian trade language are examples.[24] From the Choctaw's lingua franca, some say, we borrowed the "all-American" word *okay*, which is now probably the world's best-known word.[25] The rough equality suggested here is like the idea of reciprocal and tolerant *convivencia*, or coexistence, presumably indicated by the "Two Row Wampum Belt" (*kaswehntha*) with which the Iroquois welcomed the Europeans to their territory (1620): "We will not be like father and son, but like brothers.

These two rows [of darker shells] symbolize vessels, traveling down the same river together. One will be for the Original People, their laws, their customs, and the other for the European people and their laws and customs. We will each travel the river together, but each in our own boat. And neither of us will try to steer the other's vessel."[26] It is no wonder that Governor De Witt Clinton argued that the Iroquois confederates were "the Romans of the West."[27]

Where there is an *outright* colonial situation of the sort that the Iroquois themselves sought to avoid, however, pidgins of a different sort often arise even more readily. Concerning the colonial situation in the Belgian Congo, for example, Johannes Fabian writes the following: "The term *vehicular trade language* is made to apply to the kind of language one would expect, e.g., *Bangala* [a so-called trade language, associated with Lingala and Mangala, spoken still in what we might call Haut-Zaïre] but also to European languages which could have a vehicular function; native languages . . . could include autochthonous as well as vehicular languages, provided they were of African origin." Often, Fabian says, "the national language problem [here he is referring to the Congo] is bypassed by never mentioning French or Flemish, let alone asking for a choice between the two"[28]—much as, in the United States, there is still no official language.

Is there Native American writing? Would it be Incan knotted cords? Mayan hieroglyphic codices? Ojibwa grave posts? Mi'kmaq hieroglyphs? Wampum?[29] The ongoing debate about such questions involves issues of a potential syncretism between European and Indian use of pictures and letters in religious interaction, mapmaking, and money transaction.[30] William Johnson, in his *North American Indians* (1772), wrote that wampum belts are "as records of public transactions" (figs. 55 and 56).[31] A photograph of Iroquois chiefs from the Six Nations Reserve, taken in present-day Ontario, shows them "reading" wampum belts from the 1870s. (See frontispiece; the photograph includes an image of one of Johnson's descendants.) Thomas Carlyle observed (1830), "History has been written with quipo-threads, with feather pictures, with wampum-belts."[32] Europeans themselves included wampum in treaties as interlinguistic translations—so Lydekker reminds us in *Faithful Mohawks*.[33] In much the same spirit, Native Americans demanded written English, French, or Dutch copies of meeting minutes (plate 8).[34] Hoffman, in his *Beginnings of Writing* (1895), argued that wampum was intended to do more than aid the memory—which is the simpler task that Parkman usually assigned to it.[35] Lubbock, in 1865, called wampum a "supplement" to the American Indians' "art of picture-writing."[36]

In fact, the American colonists and European traders studied wampum belts as if they were simple pictographic texts, placing a representation of an actual wampum belt on the left-hand side of a page and its deciphering, or "translation," on the right. One example involves a wampum friendship collar (fig. 57) given in 1778 by the Iroquois of Kahnawake (in Québec) to the Mi'kmaqs of Restigouche (in New Brunswick).[37] Scholars also often show how to "translate" wampum counting and accounting, as in Bonneville's *De l'Amérique et des Américains* (1772)

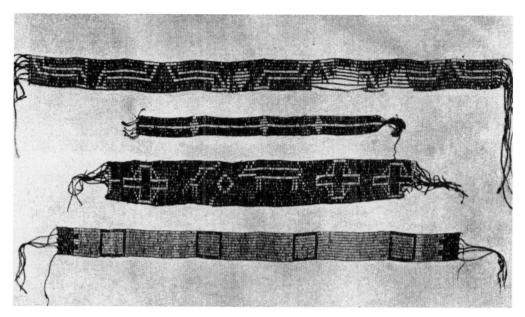

55. Wampum belts. The "Four Nations Alliance." Eighteenth century. From Horatio Hale, "Four Huron Wampum Records: A Study of Aboriginal American. History of Mnemonic Symbols," *Journal of the Royal Anthropological Institute of Great Britain and Ireland* 26 (1897), plate 11, number 4.

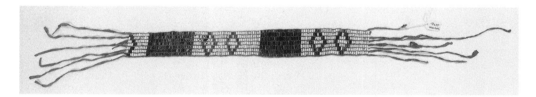

56. Wampum belt. Said to have been obtained in Nova Scotia. Photo courtesy National Museum of the American Indian, Smithsonian Institution (018677). Photo by NMAI Photo Services Staff.

(fig. 58).[38] Both Indian and colonial diplomats would often send out, in one pouch, "a Letter and Belt and String and Very Agreeable Speeches." Envoys "routinely had paper in one pocket and wampum—tagged and numbered to correspond to particular written speeches—in the other."[39] The Algonquian writing systems of the Lenape, or Delaware, tribes provide a probably counterfeit reproduction of the term for "wampum-maker" (fig. 59).

In the eighteenth century, there were many professional wampum translators. Sir William Johnson, who had been so employed, provides a relevant report (1771) noting that

> the Inds use Sticks as well to Express the alliance of Castles as the number of Individuals in a party. These Sticks are generally ab[out]t 6 Inches in length & very slender & painted Red if the Subject is War but without any peculiarity as to Shape. Their belts are mostly

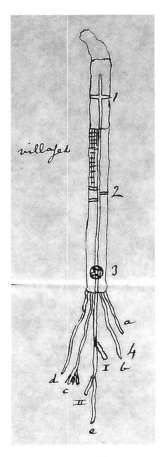

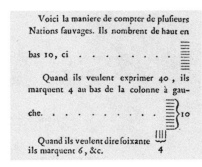

58. Detail. Explanation of numbering in wampum. 1722. From Zacharie de Pazzi de Bonneville, *De l'Amérique et des Américains, ou observations curieuses du philosophe La Douceur* (Berlin: Samuel Pitram, 1772), 86. Photo courtesy HCL-Houghton.

Voici la maniere de compter de plufieurs Nations fauvages. Ils nombrent de haut en bas 10, ci . . . .

Quand ils veulent exprimer 40 , ils marquent 4 au bas de la colonne à gau-che. . . . . }10

Quand ils veulent dire foixante ils marquent 6 , &c. 4

57. Drawing. Detail. Friendship belt. 1778. Musée de la civilisation, Archives du Séminaire de Québec, photograph by Idra Labrie, no. SME9/305/42B.

59. "The Tally Maker." 1833. *Walum Olum.* 1833. Lenape: "Sagimawtenk olumapi, leksahown sohalawak." English: "After him, Tally-Maker, who made records." "Walum Olum, or Red-Score, of the Lenâpé," in *The Multilingual Anthology of American Literature: A Reader of Original Texts with English Translations,* ed. Marc Shell and Werner Sollors (New York: New York University Press, 2000), 4.23. See also Daniel G. Brinton, *The Lenâpé and Their Legends: With the Complete Text and Symbols of the Walam-Olum, a New Translation, and an Inquiry into its Authenticity* (Philadelphia: the author, 1885), 192, 193.

black Wampum, painted red when they denote War, they describe Castles sometimes upon them as square figures of White Wampum, & in Alliances Human figures holding a Chain of friendship, each figure represents a nation, an axe is also sometimes described wh[i]c[h] is always an Emblem of War. The Taking it up is a Declaration [of war] and the burying it a token of Peace.[40]

If wampum is "the symbol of the power of the word," as some modern writers aver, then we ought to take literally the saying of Hiawatha, often repeated during the first decades of the twentieth century, that "the strings [for the wampum beads] would become words."[41] It is worth

60. Banknote. Cherokee. One dollar. 1862.
Issued during the Civil War by the Cherokee
Nation and redeemable in Confederate
currency. From Fred Reinfeld, *The Story of
Civil War Money* (New York: Sterling, 1959), 61.

emphasizing here that the Cherokee Nation
had an openly acknowledged public syllabary
by 1825. (This was thanks either to Sequoyah's
invention of that syllabary or to his bringing to
light a long-existent priestly one.) The Cherokees had their own native language newspaper

61. Coin. Salt Lake City, Utah. Gold.
Five dollars. 1860. Imprinted using the
Deseret writing system of the Mormons.
Translation: "Holiness to the Lord." Probably
engraved by J. M. Barlow. CS.

in the 1820s.[42] Most important for our present purposes, the Cherokees were issuing their own
regular paper money in a manner that adapted their earlier ongoing exchange systems to a different technology and new uses (fig. 60).

This Cherokee paper money uses the roman alphabet, at a time when some European
Americans were using Indian-style symbols. The Mormons of the early period identified so
closely with New World peoples, whom they regarded as lost tribes of Israel, that they composed a New World alphabet of their own. This "Deseret" system appears on their coined
money, as in a five-dollar gold piece of 1860 (fig. 61, plate 16). The new alphabet worried
the American authorities, especially federal officials, who were concerned with *foreign* legal
tender in the United States. They called the Deseret system "cabalistic." In the country's annual and official mint reports, they castigated the Mormons in the same terms that they used
to disparage the Indians.[43]

Words are a consequential part of a people's culture. Just how consequential in America? North
American Indian languages were once the chief focus of debates and considerations about "the
linguistic construction of reality" and about whether we can ever understand the thought of
people whose language is different from our own.[44] The German-American Whorf's book *Language, Thought, and Reality* may seem nowadays to suggest that it hardly matters that a language
disappears because we could never have really learned it in the first place.[45] Since supposedly
"you can't think about what you don't talk about," our idea of wampum—mere "social con-

struction"—is all we have.[46] Similarly, half-forgotten Native American semiotic systems might be sign language and drum language. Drum language was explicitly banned, later to appear as the complex percussions of mainstream jazz. The word *wampum* was silently absorbed,[47] later to become the often unrecognized and still unacknowledged remnants of an Indian semiology still informing our own monetary complex and syntax.

Consider Henry Wadsworth Longfellow's poem *Hiawatha* (1855)—the name means "seeker after wampum," as Benjamin Franklin Decosta stresses in his *Hiawatha; or, The Story of the Iroquois Sage* (1873).[48] Soon after its extraordinarily successful publication in the 1850s, Longfellow's remarkable poetic elaboration and assimilation of Native American wampum folklore was translated into many New World languages, including Ojibwa.[49] The Ojibwa, having half-forgotten their own traditions, translated Longfellow's poem into Ojibwa—"back" into their own language. Is it an accident that Longfellow was, institutionally speaking, the de facto founder of the academic field of comparative literature in the United States?[50] Not surprisingly, the term *wampum keeper* (= *hiawatha*) in American public discourse was soon to become part of a multifaceted notion of American national identity at once pro-Indian and profoundly assimilationist.[51] On the one hand was the twentieth-century universalist Improved Order of Red Men, a fraternal organization with a largely European-American membership.[52] On the other hand was the Indian Council Fire, with its largely 1920s Chicago-style Indian membership who called their treasurer a "wampum-keeper."[53] The culmination of racialist stereotyping is often the composite incarnation of the stereotype into one's own thought and practice.

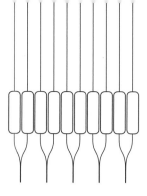

CHAPTER EIGHT

Civilization

Wampum and many European-style monies are not all that different. On the one hand, there is the view, already reported by Captain John Smith in his *Generall Historie of Virginia* (1624), that "rawranoke [roanoke] or white beads . . . occasion as much dissention among the Salvages, as gold and silver amongst Christians."[1] (Smith was rescued by the "Indian maiden" Pocahontas, whose later baptism is memorialized in the huge painting *Baptism of Pocahontas at Jamestown, Virginia* [1840], which hangs in the rotunda of the United States Capitol and is reproduced on National Bank notes [fig. 62, plate 12].) On the other hand is the fact that Europeans found it very easy to learn about currency from the Indians. It is true enough that "conquest of the barbarians was part of the taming of the wilderness," as Louis Martin Sears puts it in the allegedly "scientific" *American Journal of Sociology*.[2] As often happens, however, the "Savages" or barbarians in the New World were doing taming of their own, albeit without the apparent economic and military success of the self-nominated conquerors.

From the start, wampum redeemed the commercial traffic in the New World from mere barter. Thomas Jefferson himself warns us to beware any simple opposition between "European" and "Savage" when it comes to barter and such apparently fiduciary monetary systems

62. National Bank note. First Charter Period. Twenty dollars. 1863–75. Detail, showing Pocahontas being baptized in 1613. American Numismatic Association Money Museum.

as wampum. One example involves his relevant correspondence with President John Adams. Jefferson knew that Adams called any paper money that was not fully backed by specie "a cheat upon somebody" and, having just founded the University of Virginia, made an ironic plea for public instruction in the ways of private and public finance.[3]

> The evils of this deluge of paper money are not to be removed until our citizens are gener-ally and radically instructed in their cause and consequences, and silence by their authority the interested clamors and sophistry of speculating, shaving, and banking institutions. Till then, we must be content to return *quoad hoc* [to this extent] to the savage state, to recur to barter in the exchange of our property for want of a stable common measure of value, that now in use [paper] being less fixed than the beads and wampum of the Indian, and to deliver up our citizens, their property and their labor, passive victims to the swindling tricks of bankers and mountebankers.[4]

Perhaps Indian currencies could mediate usefully between European-style sophistry and barter exchange in the nineteenth century. Among the American colonists in the early seventeenth century, certainly, the sort of wampum to which Jefferson here refers had come into legitimate legal use as something like foreign legal tender and was already becoming an informing factor in American civilization. Not surprisingly, the Europeans had uneasy and often insightful no-tions about their early commercial meetings with and learning from the various Indian tribes, not least of all when it came to wampum.

Many earlier encounters involved theoretical problems of language (linguistic translation) and trade (monetary conversion).[5] When it came to certain kinds of wampum, linguistic and economic go-betweens on both sides were astute at "memoriz[ing] the speech on wampum belts."[6] The encounters themselves are often memorialized.

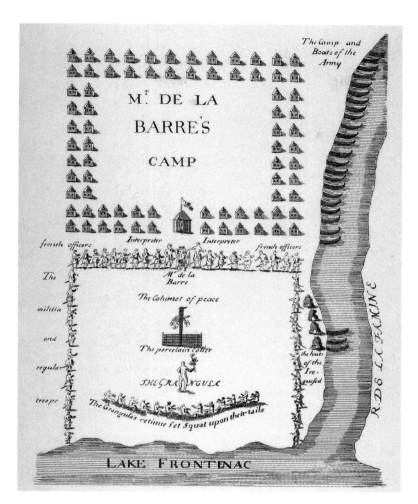

The following text appears within the engraving:

The Camp and Boats of the Army

M.ͬ DE LA BARRE'S

CAMP

french officers   Interpreter   Interpreter   french officers

The

militia

and

regular

troops

M.ͬ de la Barre

The Calumet of peace

The porcelain collier

the huts of the Iro-quoise

THE GRANGULA

The Grangula's retinue set Squat upon their tails

R. DE LA FAMINE

LAKE FRONTINAC

63. Engraving. The Military Encampments of Le Febvre de La Barre and of Grangula [Big Mouth], September 5, 1684, at La Famine. 1703. Drawn by Baron de Lahontan. Beauchamp 282.

One intercultural meeting took place on September 5, 1684, at La Famine, on the south shore of Lake Ontario.[7] This was during the invasion of Mohawk country by the French governor, Joseph-Antoine Le Febvre de La Barre, and the Onondaga orator-chief "Big Mouth" was there, helping to mediate between the French and the Senecas.[8] An illustration provided by Baron de Lahontan—who much influenced Montesquieu, Voltaire, and Jonathan Swift—depicts the wampum belt (*porcelain collier*) as the articulating center for the treaty (fig. 63).[9]

Jacques de Meulles describes this meeting in a letter to the French navy secretary, Jean-Baptiste Antoine Colbert, Marquis de Seignelay. Later on, in 1685, Seignelay (the son of Jean-Baptiste Colbert himself) refused to send Québec cash to pay the troops. De Meulles then "invented" playing-card money [*monnaie de carte*] on the model of wampum. He declared the new currency legal tender and protected it by means of anticounterfeiting legislation.[10] This playing-card money circulated in the French-American colony from 1685 to 1719 and from 1729 to 1757, oftentimes despite the French king's halfhearted attempts to suppress it.[11]

The Jesuit Frenchman Joseph-François Lafitau, who worked at Kahnawake in Québec, also provides descriptions of wampum meetings. Lafitau, a founder of modern comparative anthropology, points out, in his pathbreaking *Moeurs des sauvages amériquains* (1724), that one Indian word for wampum is *garihoua* (literally, "an item of business"). He then argues that, among the First Peoples of the New World, there *cannot* be any transaction without wampum. Only then does Lafitau provide his descriptions of traditional wampum readings (fig. 64).[12] Anglophone writers too report "the reading of the wampum" at Indian meetings. For example, the Moravian Englishman John Heckewelder, who worked among the Delaware tribes-people, describes wampum as a "speech-bag."[13]

In 1690, five years after the beginning of the French experiment with playing-card money, the British-American colony of Massachusetts, after having failed to take Québec, paid its troops with paper money, and thereafter it continued to issue paper despite the English king's many attempts to stop it.[14] The Anglo-American colonists' own general fears about economic and linguistic first encounters, especially in regard to wampum, are suggested, almost sardonically, on the paper money that they eventually issued in the New World. Among later examples are the banknotes from Georgia that show James Oglethorpe's treaty with the Creeks and/or Muskogee in 1733 (fig. 65), the same year that forty-two Sephardic Jews arrived at the Savannah Colony. Another example is the banknote from Syracuse, New York (fig. 66), that shows the Treaty at Fort Stanwix (1768).

64. Lithograph. 1724. Five Nations representatives in a council meeting at the time of the French Jesuit Joseph-François Lafitau's eighteenth-century expedition into Iroquois territory. A wampum belt stands at the forefront. From Lafitau's *Moeurs des sauvages amériquains comparées aux moeurs des premiers temps* (Paris: Saugrain l'aîné, C. E. Hochereau, 1724). Photo courtesy HCL–Houghton.

65. Banknote vignette. James Oglethorpe's treaty as it appears on the fifty-dollar bill from the Marine Bank of Georgia, Savannah. Durand p. 6.

66. Banknote vignette. Treaty at Fort Stanwix as it appears on the two-dollar bill from the Syracuse City Bank of Syracuse, New York. Durand p. 31.

In seventeenth-century Massachusetts, wampum was widespread as the official legal tender; for transactions under ten pounds, it was legally mandated. In 1640, the legal conversion in Massachusetts was four pence for the white and two pence for the blue (or black) *suckau*. Records show that many inventories of deceased English colonists contained wampum and no other currency.[15] However, the decisive moment of transition to the legal status of wampum occurred in the 1690s. Soldiers from Massachusetts returned home from the unsuccessful campaign to Québec and threatened to mutiny unless they received their wages. The Massachusetts mint was insufficient.[16] Therefore, Massachusetts, in crisis, came up with an expedient based partly on the French experiment with playing-card money. American soldiers serving in Québec would have witnessed firsthand the circulation of De Meulles's playing-card money. The Massachusetts colonists would issue paper money just as if it were wampum (figs. 67 and 68).[17] The British-American, or Massachusetts, colonists accepted this "paper wampum." The acceptance, with discount, was arguably the first moment in the history of genuinely widespread paper money in what is now the United States, and hence, perhaps, in the world at large.[18] It was appropriate, then, that the newly formed United States minted its 1787 and 1788 cent coins with images of the Indian from the "seal" (fig. 69, plate 11).

A similar tale might be told for the early Dutch settlers in America, especially in New Holland, now New York State. There too wampum was the first legal tender.[19] The Dutch brought to bear their own banking and linguistic traditions. Before immigrating to the New World, they had used specie for most transactions. For them, the severe shortage of specie in the New World, together with New Holland's natural wealth, was especially troubling.[20] They soon learned that shell worked as well as coin—in fact, better. The foreign legal tender that was wampum was now used for treaties, trade, cash money, and commodity. After the English occupied New Holland (1664), wampum became legal tender in the colony of New York

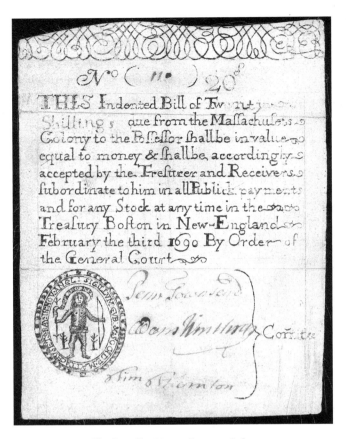

67. Banknote. Bill of credit. Massachusetts Colony
Twenty shillings. 1690. The first paper money in America.
Massachusetts Historical Society, Boston.

68. Detail, banknote.

**69. One-cent coin. Commonwealth of Massachusetts. 1787 and/or 1788.
Indian on obverse; eagle and shield with "cent" inscription on reverse.
First American coin with the cent denomination. ANS 1911.85.4 and 1911.85.4r.**

(1673). It lost its legal tender status as "foreign" tender in New York in 1701, when authorities introduced paper to fill the same need.[21]

The English Christians saw the great utility of wampum as money. However, they were worried about the proto-capitalist—and purportedly unchristian—tendencies of its use. Just such fears are traceable back to the aristocratic Plato and Aristotle's probably ineradicable suspicions of genuinely fiduciary money. Governor William Bradford, for example, who came over on the *Mayflower* (1628), even imagined that the production and use of wampum might "prove a drug in time."[22] With this reference to the New World's money as the opiate of the people, the Puritan Bradford does not so much indicate prescience about the relationship between money and tobacco[23] as he expresses an unyielding fear that the colonists would become, as it were, "savage" and "pagan." Later on, conservative colonists, vaunting the values of "civilization," oftentimes called wampum the "devil's currency."[24]

Some settlers believed that they would lose their wits to wampum even as the Indians would lose their wits to a white man's drug: liquor. Thomas Morton writes in his *New English Canaan* (1637) that the Indians "will *pawn* their wits to purchase the acquaintance of it [alcohol]."[25] His choice of the word *pawn* is worth marking. The English noun *wampe* means both "pawn" ("pledge," "deposit") *and* "wampum."[26] So, Morton's choice of words slyly suggests the association between the effects of wampum (wampe) on Europeans and those of alcohol on Indians. Later on, in fact, Americans usually tried to dismiss their own paper wampum as beneath civilized practice. In an issue of the recreational magazine *Outing* (1893) one user writes, "I laid some of their own miserable, smelly, garlicky, paper-wampum upon their official . . . desk, saying, as I did this: 'You can keep the change.'"[27]

| | | | | | | | | |

There is a marked analogy here between the role of the image of Jews and that of Indians in some American culture. For Christians back home in Europe and England, Jews had long played the role of the "money devil." As such, they had served a particular role in defining Christendom, if not the settler's own Christianity.[28] Now, in America, the few Jews got to share the stage of prejudice with the Indians. There were myriad relevant joke banknotes in the nineteenth century. An anti-Semitic joke "One Levy" banknote from around 1837 (fig. 70) bears the inscription, "Received of Dr. Faustus, ONE LEVY, being part of a deposit of Thirty Thousand, which is payable to him, with interest, at the rate of one per cent per annum, at the Chapel of the STREET GAZETTE, at the current quoin of the Bank." A penniless Benjamin Franklin is shown arriving in Philadelphia (fig. 71). At the right is a poem:

> The veriest venal in the world's high place,
>> That boasts his pride o'er fate, or change, or chance,
> Is but some creature shining by the grace
>> Of his "metallic currency of coutenance"
>>> Some base reflection in the sun's bright beams
>>> That when you grasp it is but all it seems.
>> And we, the freeman's hope, the despot's dread,
>> Support the people while we beg for bread.

In *The Last of the Mohicans*, with its various commercial encounters between Indian and colonist, James Fenimore Cooper had American culture's views right when he prominently quoted Shakespeare's Jewish money devil on behalf of the Indians: "If you deny me, fie upon your law! / There is no force in the decrees of Venice: / I stand for judgment."[29] Stanford University's Indian mascot, when I was a student there, had a very large "Jewish" nose. But it is Mormonism, that all-American creed—it is the only religion founded by Europeans in America—that best represents the alliance of Indians and Jews in American thinking.

Mormonism puts forth three interconnected views about Indians and Jews. First is the view that the Native Americans are descended from the Jews and hence Jewish. The "Introduction" to the Book of Mormon (1830), put out by the Church of Jesus Christ of Latter-day Saints, states that the "the Lamanites are the principal ancestors of the American Indians." Laman was the son of the Jewish Lehi, probably a merchant, who traveled to the Americas in 600 B.C. Historically, that is the time that Greeks and Jews in Asia Minor were experimenting with the first actual coins.[30] Second is the view that the several references to money in the Book of Mormon relate both to the ancient coinage brought by Lehi to the New World around 600 B.C. and to the wampum of the Indians.[31] The third circumstance involves the production of the Book of Mormon itself. On the one hand, that production parallels the Jewish creation of the Ten Commandments and, by extension, the Five Books of Moses. Moses engraved the commandments on the second set of tablets from dictation or memory. The language that God spoke (Hebrew, Egyptian, Midianite,

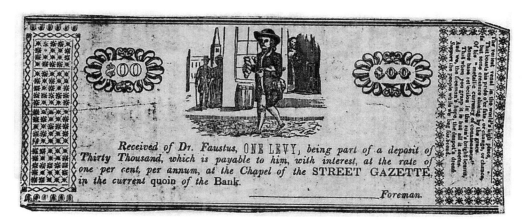

70. Cartoon. Anti-Semitic joke banknote. One Levy. Circa 1837. Rulau N23.

71. Detail, anti-Semitic joke banknote. Rulau N28.

and some form of glossolalia are all candidates) is a matter of debate, although the tablets come down to us in Hebrew.[32] The Book of Mormon states that it is "an account written by the hand of Mormon upon plates taken from the plates of Nephi [another son of Lehi]"; Joseph Smith translated it from a foreign tongue into English. On the other hand, the production of the Book of Mormon by Joseph Smith has parallels to the way that Sequoyah, the Cherokee chief, often claimed a tradition of lost golden plates on which were engraved the "original" writing, plates that, in these latter days, had been lost, hidden, or destroyed.[33]

It is worth considering here that many of the settlers' charges against the Indians seem to come as much from their own religious and economic disposition as from anything to do with the Indians. "Indian giving" is one example. Others would include scalping and cannibalism. Scalping involves the removal of skin from some animal such as a beaver or a bison, oftentimes for trading purposes. The trade in human scalps in the New World would seem to have been inspired more by the Europeans than by traditional Indian practices. Not only did they put out bounties for Indian scalps, but they first developed beaver money and, as quasi-scientific taxidermists, came to define "the soul in the skin," as does William Temple Hornaday, in *The Extermination of the American Bison* (1899).[34] Even as the Europeans and Anglo-Americans introduced the practice of scalping "tickets," so they often took "cannibalism"—of the sort to which Thomas Nast refers in his cartoon *Milk Tickets*—to be the only proper English-language translation of the Indian word *Mohawk*.[35] The mysterious projection at work here involves the

Christian Eucharist itself, which spiritualizes cannibalism: "This is my body" (*Hoc est corpus meum*), says Jesus at the Last Supper (Matthew 26:26), a ceremony remembered, along with his body, when the priest distributes coin-shaped flour disks that are then consumed by the participants. Thomas Nast recognizes this cannibalizing aspect of his civilized American neighbors by means of the specifically digestant cartoon banknote in *Milk Tickets*: the cartoon ticket depicts the dollar sign, "$," and reads, "This is Money by the Act of Cannibals." Indians were often accused of having quaint or dangerous chants and practices (*hocus pocus*), as by George Catlin in his *North American Indians* (1844).[36]

Weeden, author of *Economic and Social History of New England, 1620–1890* (1891), argued that "Indian money" was the *key* factor in New England "civilization," and, as we have already seen, designers and bankers had been both aware and wary of the fact.[37] Walter Benjamin might well have had in mind just such notes when he wrote, in his little essay "Tax Advice" (1926), that a new kind of numismatics is called for. "A descriptive analysis of bank notes is needed," he says. "The unlimited satirical force of such a book would be equaled only by its objectivity. For nowhere more naively than in these documents does capitalism display itself in solemn earnest."[38] Not all that ironically or naïvely, though, did many anglophone towns and banking companies name themselves "Wampum": Wampum, a town in Lawrence County, Pennsylvania, is only one example (fig. 72). Dozens of magazines ran stories about "the *first* American paper money,"[39] and they all liked best to reproduce early banknotes showing the insignium of the Indian (figs. 73–77).

There are very many other American banknotes with Indians on them. In the Collection Selechonek, for example, there are banknotes from hundreds of "independent" nineteenth-century banks from all over the United States. Banknotes in the first two-thirds of the nineteenth century show Indians in a large variety of poses: sitting beside white men on the banks of a river as a steamboat passes in the distance (fig. 78); standing and kneeling beside tepees (fig. 79); observing the sea from a mountain pass (fig. 80); standing beside their horses as they observe a passing rail train (fig. 81); overlooking a river town from atop a clifflike promontory; tracking wild animals; hunting buffalo; seated on a tree stump with a dog; and using a bow and arrow in such a way that the person who observes the banknote is reminded of Cupid (fig. 82).[40]

72. Banknote. Wampum Furnace Company. Wampum, Pennsylvania. Five dollars. 1867. Durand p. 118.

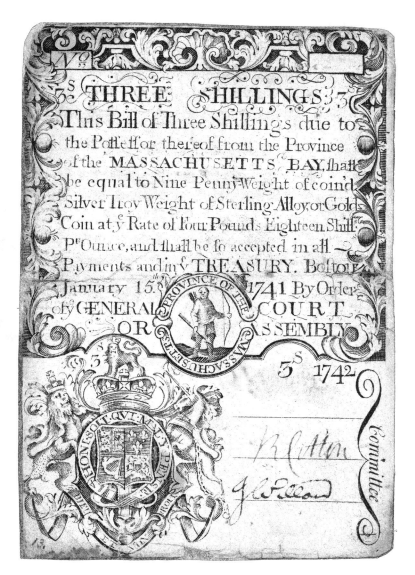

**73. Letter of credit. Province of the Massachusetts Bay.
Three shillings. 1741–42. Newman 177.**

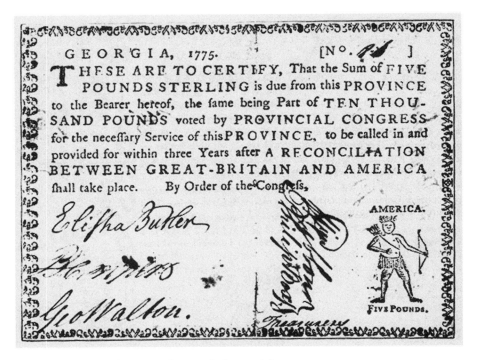

74. Banknote. Georgia. 5 pounds. 1775. In lower right: AMERICA and sketch of Indian. Newman 116.

75. Banknote. New York. Two pounds. 1760. Showing two weights, with Indian and colonist together holding crest. Printed by William Weyman. ANS 0000.999.29182.

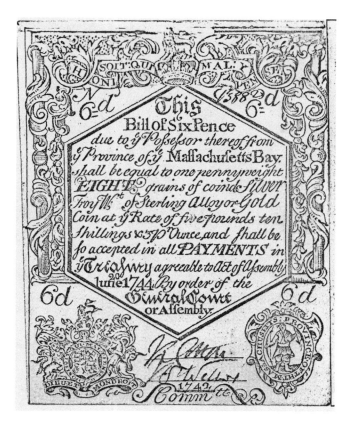

76. Banknote. Massachusetts. Six pence. 1744. Newman 178.

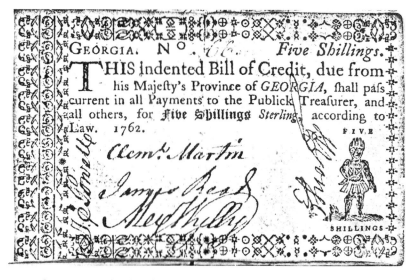

77. Banknote. Georgia. Five shillings. 1762. Newman 111.

78. Banknote. Bank of the State of Missouri at Fayette. Detail of ten-dollar note. 1830s–40s.
HMS 1901.

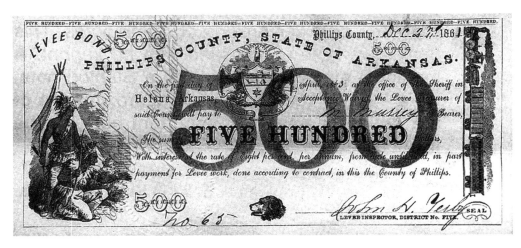

79. Phillips County levee inspector bond. Five hundred dollars.
Helena, Arkansas. December 1861. *HMS* 1619.

80. Banknote. Lord and Williams Company. Tucson, Arizona Territory.
One-dollar note. 1870s, *HMS* 1618.

81. Banknote. City Bank of Kenosha, Wisconsin. Detail of one-dollar note. 1850s.
HMS 5496. A similar image is on issues from Bank of Moneka, State of Wisconsin.

82. Banknote. City of Pensacola, Florida.
6 ¼ cents. Issued in 1838. *HMS* 1678.

83. Banknote. Alabama State Bank.
Decatur, Alabama. 1830s. Detail. *HMS* 1563.

84. Banknote. Portsmouth Bank. New Hampshire. Twenty dollars. 1830s–40s. *HMS* 1927.

85. United States military payment certificate. Portrait of Chief Ouray. Twenty dollars. Issued 1970–73.

86. United States military payment certificate. Portrait of Chief Hollow Horn Bear. Ten dollars. Issued 1970–73.

Two groups of these paper-money types deserve special attention. In examples from the first, there is a large vignette of an Indian with bow and arrow. Sometimes there is behind him (fig. 83); sometimes the arrow is aimed directly at a head of a figure of Athena or Commerce (fig. 84). The second, from a later period in American history, is composed of the various military payment certificates ("substitute money" for American military personnel serving in foreign countries) issued during the last three years of the American War in Vietnam: these notes show the Ute chief Ouray (fig. 85) and the Brulé Sioux chief Hollow Horn Bear (fig. 86).[41]

The tradition lives on.

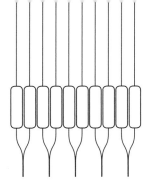

CHAPTER NINE

Wall Street and Democracy

NO ONE WHO HAS NOT HEARD THE OUTCRIES
AND HOWLINGS OF A MODERN TARSHISH,
AT ANY CHECK UPON "PAPER MONEY,"
CAN HAVE ANY IDEA OF THE CLAMOR
AGAINST PETER THE HEADSTRONG
[IN MANHATTAN'S FINANCIAL DISTRICT]
FOR CHECKING THE CIRCULATION
OF OYSTER SHELLS.

——WASHINGTON IRVING,
KNICKERBOCKER'S HISTORY OF NEW YORK (1809)

Five closely interrelated, multifaceted factors in pan-American linguistic translation and monetary conversion, taken together, need further explication when it comes to considering the notion of American identity in relation to wampum.[1] This is all the more the case when one wonders what sort of historical path there is "from wampum to Wall Street," as Elizabeth Black puts it in the familiar joking way that writers adopt when they discus wampum. (Some talk also of the path "from wampum to postal service," which is how an official Canadian publication likewise sums things up.)[2] These factors involve inflation, counterfeiting, debt, diplomacy, and democracy.

Inflation

North Americans, especially those in the Northeast, learned much from how sheer "state power" had allowed money systems to operate in Mexico and Nicaragua—by pegging rates through political tyranny.[3] More important, thanks to the importation of gold and silver from Central America, there was a profound and eventually observable change in the amounts of gold and silver in Europe. For Spain, the influx of gold made for inflation. The Spanish court seemed stupidly unable to understand the widespread "state money" that circulated in the New World apparently without benefit of any rare raw materials—thanks only to the cacao bean, say.[4] The German-national Humboldt, in his studies of precious metals, detailed the process.[5] For the United States, such studies were a major theme of Alexander Del Mar, and in that policy arena, the United States moved first.[6] Monetary power, writes Jonathan Kirshner, "is a remarkably efficient component of state power . . . the most potent instrument of economic coercion to states in a position to exercise it."[7] From observing various aspects of the wampum trade, New Netherlanders and New Englanders learned much about inflation and paper money, as Beauchamp observes (1901).[8] In this respect, as Del Mar suggests, American colonists were among the first people to understand the implications of the land-based John Law paper-money experiments in Louisiana (1720).[9] Two interrelated matters are of special concern here: inflation and the money supply.

Washington Irving, for one, takes a decidedly conservative stance toward the inflation that occurred in New Netherland in the first half of the seventeenth century. In his half-humorous *[Diedrich] Knickerbocker's History of New York* (1809), Irving describes how William Kieft, the director-general of New Netherland (1639–47), "flood[ed] the streets of New Amsterdam with Indian money." Irving's Knickerbocker says that wampum did have "an intrinsic value among the Indians, who used it to ornament their robes and moccasins," but "among the honest burghers it had no more intrinsic value than those rags which form the paper currency of modern days." He reports, "William [Kieft] the Testy, seeing this money of easy production, conceived the project of making it the current coin of the province." Things went well, for a few months anyhow. "For a time affairs went on swimmingly; money became as plentiful as in the modern days of paper currency, and, to use the popular phrase, 'a wonderful impulse was given to public prosperity.'"[10]

However, clever "Yankee traders" soon took advantage of the situation. Some used wampum to purchase goods but demanded Dutch guilders for the goods they sold. Other Yankees introduced inferior wampum to the Dutch colony. Within a short period, Irving writes, "the Yankees had made a descent upon Long Island, and had established a kind of mint at Oyster Bay, where they were coining up all the oyster banks." Irving draws the conclusion for the future of the North American continent: "Thus early did the knowing men of the East [New England] manifest their skill in bargaining the New Amsterdammers [*sic*] out of the oyster, and leaving them the shell."[11] Bad money drives out good; increasing the money supply can make for prosperity; too much makes for inflation. (One of the vignettes in Irving's *Money-Diggers*— "Wolfert Webber, or Golden Dreams" [1824], set on Manhattan Island—makes much the same point in the realms of narratological aesthetics and monetary economics.)[12]

Actually, the Dutch traders helped to precipitate the inflation. They supplied the Indians with metal tools whereby they increased the rate of production of wampum; they also manufactured their own wampum in the same way as the English.

When Peter Stuyvesant took over the directorship of New Netherland (1647), Irving reports that he "had old-fashioned notions in favor of gold and silver, which he considered the true standards of wealth and mediums of commerce, and one of his first edicts was that all duties to government should be paid in those precious metals, and that seawant, or wampum, should no longer be a legal tender." This meant that "all those who speculated on the rise and fall of this fluctuating currency found their calling at an end; those, too, who had hoarded Indian money by barrels full, found their capital shrunk in amount; but, above all, the Yankee traders, who were accustomed to flood the market with newly-coined oyster-shells, and to abstract Dutch merchandise in exchange, were loud-mouthed in decrying this 'tampering with the currency.'" Irving properly draws the analogy to paper money: "No one who has not heard the outcries and howlings of a modern Tarshish [a wealthy city in biblical accounts], at any check upon 'paper money,' can have any idea of the clamor against Peter the Headstrong [Stuyvesant] for checking the circulation of oyster-shells."[13]

Americans learned in Long Island that he who controls the money supply wins the war. The historian Peter Ross writes of Oyster Bay, "The English held it; the Dutch claimed it; so it was a sort of no-man's land."[14] Whether or not it makes any sense to call the Pequots "no-one," the Dutch and English certainly did face off at Oyster Bay.[15] Louis Jordan writes, "The Dutch were strategically placed to control the fur trade. They controlled the Hudson River which gave them easy access to the Indian tribes who collected the furs. Additionally, with the establishment of their capital of New Amsterdam on the southern tip of the Island of Manhattan and the building [in 1624] of Fort Amsterdam, they controlled the sea port necessary for foreign trade. Also, and equally as important, New Amsterdam was located in the regional center for wampum production."[16]

Cornelis van Tienhoven, the secretary of New Netherland, wrote that "the greatest part of the Wampum, for which the furs are traded, is manufactured there [Long Island] by the Natives." He added, "This point [on Long Island] is also well adapted to secure the trade of the Indians in Wampum (the mine of New Netherland) since in and about the abovementioned sea and the islands therein situated lie the cockles whereof Wampum is made, from which great profit could be realized by those who would plant a colony or hamlet at the aforesaid Point, for the cultivation of the land, for raising all sorts of cattle, for fishing and the wampum trade."[17] Adriaen Cornelissen van der Donck, New Amsterdam's first lawyer, claimed that *all* of Long Island should be retained by New Netherland. "Otherwise," he wrote, "the trade will suffer great damage, because the English will retain all the Wampum manufacturers to themselves and we shall be obligated to eat oats out of English hands."[18]

By the relevant treaty between the Dutch and English (1650), all land east of the west side of Oyster Bay was granted to the English, and all land west to the Dutch.[19] Eventually, Stuyvesant ceded all New Netherland to the English (1664). The anglophone path from Wampum Beach to Wall Street was already underway. (The Dutch learned their lesson and tried to apply it in colonies of their own elsewhere.)

Counterfeiting

Most Europeans believed that counterfeiting was always bad for the sovereign nation. Many Americans, however, came to see from their own colonial experience that counterfeiting, as the British Crown had defined it, might help the nation—by increasing the money supply—regardless of the merely venal motives or selfish intentions of individual counterfeiters or counterfeiting gangs.

One of the American models here was, in part, the practice of several American Indian tribes, who were, in certain circumstances, willing and able to take "manufactured wampum" for economic as well as aesthetic purposes.[20] The Dutch started such wampum factories in Albany; the British did so in Massachusetts; and various Indian nations and tribes also set them up (figs. 87 and 88). English colonists too introduced imitations of wampum; the Indians easily told the difference, but they usually took the counterfeit shells near par. Hale suggests that "that which finally gave the English [and other manufactured] beads the advantage was not the superiority or cheapness of the workmanship, but the destruction [by genocide and disease, during the first half of the eighteenth century] of the Indian workmen."[21]

What was apparently straightforward counterfeiting in the eyes of the Crown—namely, the use of wampum and paper, which were often confused with each other as media of exchange—turned out to be one of the greatest monetary (and semiotic) experiments in world history. Already in his *New English Canaan* (1637), Thomas Morton argued that wampum beads "passed current as money in all parts of New England from one end of the coast to the other," with little account for manufactured or counterfeit beads.[22]

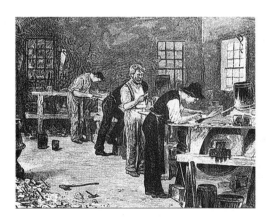

87. Frank M. Gregory. *The Four Wampum Makers.* Wood engraving. 1886. From John C. Ewers, "Hair Pipes in Plains Indian Adornment: A Study in Indian and White Ingenuity," Anthropological Paper 50, *Bureau of American Ethnology Bulletin 164* (Washington, D.C.: Government Printing Office, 1957), plate 15B. Photo courtesy HCL.

Debt

How the American Revolution was dependent on money and the Indians is sometimes hinted at on the printed faces of paper money. In the center of one vignette, for example, there is a group of tepees with General Washington, on horseback, receiving a bag of money, apparently from Ceres, goddess of agriculture (fig. 89). In later versions of this vignette, Washington receives a document instead of the money bag. One might recall, however, the painter Constanino Brumidi's ceiling mural *Apotheosis of George Washington* (1875), which is 180 feet

88. Campbell shell-drilling machine. Nineteenth century. Justin Barnum, photographer. Photo courtesy Pascack Historical Society, Park Ridge, N.J.

89. Banknote. Citizens Union Bank. Scituate, Rhode Island. Detail. Washington receiving donation from Ceres. Twenty dollars. 1840s. *HMS* 5537.

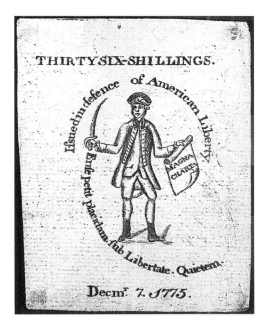

THIRTY SIX-SHILLINGS.

Issued in defence of American Liberty.

Ense petit placidam, sub Libertate, Quietem.

Decm.ʳ 7. 1775.

90. Paper money. Massachusetts. Thirty-six shillings. 1775. Engraved and printed by Paul Revere pursuant to the Resolve of August 6, 1775, and the Act of August 23, 1775. The figure holds a scroll bearing the words MAGNA CHARTA. The inscription framing the figure reads: ISSUED IN DEFENCE OF AMERICAN LIBERTY. ENSE PETIT PLACIDAM, SUB LIBERTATE, QUIETEM (By arms he seeks peace with freedom). Newman 182.

above the floor of the rotunda of the Capitol in Washington, D.C. Here Mercury, god of commerce, hands a bag of money to Robert Morris, financier of the American Revolution and cofounder of the new nation's first national bank, the Bank of North America.

The American Revolution was essentially about counterfeiting and national credit understood as such.[23] That is the argument first proposed by Del Mar in the nineteenth century and, long after him, by John Kenneth Galbraith and then by both James E. Ferguson and William G. Anderson.[24] Joseph Green's broadside *A Mournful Lamentation on the Death of Paper Money* (1781) had it right: "He [paper money] rais'd and paid our Armies brave. To guard our threaten'd State."[25] Not only did paper money finance the revolution against King George; paper money, issued precisely in defense of liberty, was the cultural and material sine qua non of the revolution. Here too, Paul Revere had it right on the paper monies he printed up (fig. 90). "Paper wampum" not only enabled the Revolution, it *was* the Revolution.

"Money is coined liberty."[26] When he wrote these words in his *Notes from the House of the Dead* in the early 1860s, the Russian writer Dostoevsky was thinking about the involuntary individual economic debt that had landed him in prison and not about the voluntary group debt that oftentimes leads to liberty. Shared fiduciary monies, like those in revolutionary France and the United States, are almost a precondition for political liberty. The eventual worthlessness of French assignats and American continentals ("not worth a continental") is, in that sense, the price of liberty.

"Give me liberty or give me death!" Patrick Henry's words in the speech known as "The War Inevitable" (1775) seem to mean that life without liberty is not worth living and that liberty is worth the price of death.[27] In this linguistic register, national willingness to risk death and take on debt—*death*'s homonym is *debt,* as Henry's oral presentation would have made clear—matches the revolutionary requirement of liberty.[28] The risk of accepting paper money was great: *Exitus in Dubio Est* (the end is in doubt) reads one of Benjamin Franklin's paper money inscriptions.[29] A powerful political bond developed among those willing to accept the risk. It is misleading to focus narrowly, as Beard often does in his *Economic Interpretation of the Constitution of the United States* (1941), on how many signers of the Constitution were public creditors who simply hoped the Constitution would raise the value of their own holdings.[30]

National debt is something not only to bemoan but also to celebrate, as Thomas Paine does. "Wampum paper," or paper money in various forms, allowed conceiving the nation-state as the common debt as well as the commonwealth of the people. Thus, Thomas Paine writes in *Common Sense* (1776), "No nation ought to be without a debt" because "a national debt is a national bond."[31] Understanding independent nationhood in terms of the language of debt had been an ongoing American business for over a century. In this perspective, it is hardly surprising that the British Crown should have been concerned about the widespread production and use of paper monies in the colonies from the 1690s until the Revolution.

In retrospect, the relevant sequence of events from the mid-eighteenth century seems almost inexorable. In *1751*: the British parliament again prohibits the New England states from making their paper currency into legal tender and maligns such currency as "mere wampum"; *1764*: the "Currency Act" forbids *all* the colonies to use paper money; *1765*: the "Stamp Act," passed by the British parliament, places a special tax on (all) printed paper. The colonists were not only unhappy that George III was raising money without the approval of colonial legislatures—whence the celebrated slogan "No taxation without representation"—they were also aware that the Stamp Act was mandating a tax on printed *paper money*. The printing of that money was already largely illegal, but the act would now make the use and distribution of such paper easier to track.

In 1765, Patrick Henry put forth fully seven resolutions against the Stamp Act. The American Revolution of 1776—together with its tea-party rebels (reacting partly to the "Tea Act" of 1773) dressed as Indians—was a long time in coming. In popular literature of the period, there are often Indians who, one way or another, watch over or oversee the finances of the Revolution. That is true especially in many of the political cartoons of the years immediately following the Stamp Act and during the revolutionary period itself.

One cartoon from 1783, Humphreys's *The Tea-Tax-Tempest, or Old Time with his Magick-Lanthern* (plate 9), emblematizes—"projects" as a series of "moving shadows"—the already mythic role that Indians played in the political and cultural foundation of the United States. This cartoon retells and foretells the American Revolution. The colonies assumed the right to print paper monies on tax-free paper. The relation between public finance and the democratic revolution in the New World is emphasized. The globe, depicted as the magic lantern, suggests possibilities for the world at large. The instigator of the whole "affair" is the stamped paper, the paper money, that inflames the boiling teakettle. The commonplace allegorical figure of Time tells us almost all:

> Here you see the little Hot Spit Fire Tea pot that has done all The Mischief. —There You see the Old British Lion basking before the American Bon Fire whilst the French Cock is blowing up a Storm about his Ears to Destroy him and his young Welpes. —There You See Miss America grasping at the Cap of Liberty. —There you see the British Forces be yok'd

and be cramp'd flying before the Congress Men—There you see the thirteen Stripes and Rattlesnake exalted.—There you see the Stamp'd Paper help to make the Pot Boil.—There you see etc. etc. etc.

Framing all is the spectator Indian. A century later, *The Tea-Tax-Tempest* still compared appropriately with the comic shadow in Thomas Nast's *A Shadow Is Not a Substance* (1876) (see figure 40).

American government officials debated the issue of whether and how to tax Indians, especially the Six Nations, without giving them proper representation.[32] The argument found its way into the textual weaving of various wampum belts, including the one called "Wing or Dust Fan of the President of Six Nations."[33]

Diplomacy

Wampum diplomacy and transactions were crucial to negotiating successfully with Indian tribes and thus not only to defining but also to carrying out the American Revolutionary War. Even in such places as Pennsylvania, which was founded too late to experience firsthand the Long Island "wampum rush" and the use of wampum as domestic and foreign legal tender, the use of wampum belts and strings was crucial to diplomacy. In 1700, for example, William Penn handed wampum to visiting Iroquois "in token of amitie & friendship wt ym [with them]."[34] Pennsylvanians became so steeped in wampum culture that when the Indian runner Satcheecho returned in August 1722 from his second trip to Onondaga concerning the murder of the Indian Sawantaeny, William Keith, Pennsylvania's governor, claimed that he was "surprised to see you bring no [wampum] Credentials with you." By the close of the colonial era, Pennsylvanians had grown so attached to the medium of wampum for diplomatic purposes that they sent wampum belts to "Iroquoia" explaining the Stamp Act crisis (1765).[35] That too is a subject of Humphreys's *The Tea-Tax-Tempest*.

George Washington knew that the outcome of the Revolutionary War depended on whether various Native American tribes chose the American or English side. "A united force of Indian warriors could either support or crush the Revolution," Washington said, admitting too, "I am a little embarrassed to know in what Manner to conduct myself with respect to the . . . Indians."[36] Congress wanted to woo the Indians. What to do?

"Without Wampum," one colonist observed in 1756, "Nothing is to be done Amongst the Indians."[37] American leaders found useful precedent in the Wampum Treaty (1682) between William Penn and Chief Tamanend of the Lenape. (That treaty, also called "The Holy Experiment," is the subject of Hezekiah Butterworth's historical novel *The Wampum Belt, or The Fairest Page of History* [1924].)[38] Washington convinced George Morgan, an expert in "wampum diplomacy," to oversee negotiations with the Indians. All Morgan's communications with the Indians were accompanied by wampum.[39] Under order from John Hancock, for example, Morgan took a wampum belt with thirteen diamond shapes (one for each colony) and twenty-five hundred wampum beads to the sachems of the western Indian nations in 1776.[40] Morgan met

Chief Guyashusta with a similarly impressive diamond wampum belt and sent it to the Grand Council of the Iroquois Six Nations.[41] As part of the attempt to provide "Union" among tribes whose political organization he much admired, Morgan sent wampum belts to the chiefs of the Shawnee and other tribes.[42]

The various peoples immigrating to the northeastern part of North America gradually learned about the use of wampum in diplomacy as in trade, and sometimes even without much experience with wampum's operation as legal tender. Pennsylvania in the 1740s, for example, had not had the chance to experiment with currencies in the way that New York and Massachusetts had done. Yet Pennsylvanians produced hundreds of wampum belts and negotiated with the Indians, and sometimes even among themselves, by means of them. Merrell writes, "From this confidence [with the use of wampum that they had learned from the Indians] came [the Pennsylvanian settlers'] desire to experiment with [the] form [of the wampum belts that they had made for their use]; some Pennsylvania belts bore decidedly non-native designs as colonists added touches of their own. Instead of hands or diamonds, belts might [now] display the Penn family crest or a provincial fort." An important transformation, to which we will return, involved the use of roman lettering. Merrell tells us, "Instead of paths or hearts [for insignia], they sported dates or initials immortalizing everyone from King George (*G R*) and Teedyuscung [Tedyuskung] (*D K,* for Delaware King) to a provincial army officer (*W C,* for [Colonel] William Clapham])."[43] This change involved more than diplomacy understood in the narrow sense. Such wampum of the political sort came to make trade possible.[44] In certain conflicts—King George's War (1744–48), the French and Indian War (1756–63), and the Seven Years' War (1756–63)—it proved invaluable.

Democracy

The English in America learned from the already centuries-old Iroquois Confederacy about how to form a more-or-less republican union.[45] One modern commentator summarized this development by observing, "Western democracy [at least in America] began with the Iroquois wampum belt."[46] The Hiawatha Wampum Belt, which enabled and still signals the Iroquois Confederacy, is, by this (common) account, "one of the original documents of human agreement in North America."[47] Certainly, that was the view around the Mohawk reserve at Kahnawake when I went to high school near Montréal.[48] The Hiawatha Belt is still much used on Native American flags and other items. Hail, therefore, Hiawatha! As noted earlier, his name means "seeker after Wampum," and Longfellow tells us that he "learned of every bird its language."[49] Henry Rowe Schoolcraft reminds us, "In his fight with the great wampum prince . . . [Hiawatha was] counseled by woodpecker to know where the vulnerable point of his antagonist lies"—as befits the founder of any republican confederacy.[50]

The Mohawk viewpoint on this matter dovetails with writings of Ben Franklin.[51] Franklin used Iroquois covenant chain imagery in designing the two-thirds dollar (1776, fig. 91) and for paper money of Georgia and elsewhere (1777, fig. 92).[52] Franklin was also one of the great backers of the American paper money project. His relevant works include *A Modest Enquiry into the Nature and Necessity of a Paper-Currency* (1729).[53] Franklin's *Copy of a Letter from Quebeck in Canada to a pr—e-m—r in France* (1747), which "purport[s] to deal with Canadian affairs," is, as Clarence William Miller suggests, "in fact a sly attack on the opponents of the use of paper currency in the colonies."[54] Franklin's own press—the same one that published *A Modest Enquiry*—printed a good deal of the paper money that circulated in the colonies.

Other "Founding Fathers" also found precedent in the Indian model for confederation. In a letter to James Madison, Thomas Jefferson writes, "A tractable people may be governed in

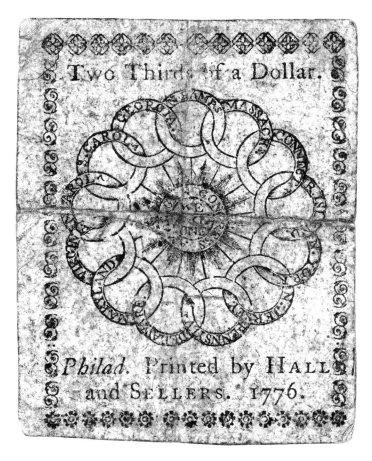

91. Banknote. Philadelphia. Two-thirds of a dollar. 1776. Continental currency. Shows covenant chain with each former colony as one link. This forms a basis for the famous 1787 FURIO cent. ANS 1989.44.2.

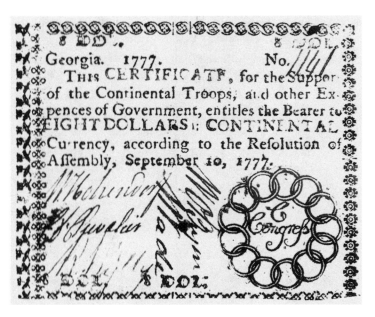

92. Banknote. Georgia. Eight dollars. 1777. The chain emblem
was adopted from Benjamin Franklin's design. Newman 127.

large bodies but, in proportion as they depart from this character, the extent of their government must be less. We see into what small divisions the Indians [other than the Iroquois] are
obliged to reduce their societies."[55]

Many Anglo-Americans regarded the Iroquois Covenant Wampum Belt as the New World's
Magna Carta.[56] The American colonials' association of wampum with British-style liberty, as that
was defined in part by the Magna Carta (A.D. 1215), helps to explain Paul Revere's prominent
display of that Old World document on the paper money he printed. Those monies had the
inscription "Issued in defence of American Liberty" (see figure 90).

The historical accuracy of claims that the Indian political organization and wampum, or
colonial understandings of them, affected the course of American political history by way of
providing a model for the American colonial union is, of course, much debated.[57] However, it
is worth pointing out three relevant factors.

First: Many early anglophone American colonists remarked on the Indian love for liberty.
Colden wrote in his *History of the Five Nations* (1727), "The Five Nations have such absolute
Notions of Liberty that they allow no kind of Superiority of one over another, and banish all
Servitude from their Territories." He was already writing in an old tradition with good histori-
cal and political bases.[58]

Second: The American-English term *caucus,* which suggests an American-style political
grouping, occurs already in Captain Smith's *Generall Historie of Virginia* (1624).[59] Trumbull suggests in *On Some Words Derived from Languages of North American Indians* (1872) that the term is

basically Algonquian. *Cau'-cau-as'u* means "one who advises, urges, encourages."[60] The caucus is, of course, that superficially undemocratic institution "which prevails in America in regard to elections," as Campbell, writing about the American spirit, puts it in his *White and Black: The Outcome of a Visit to the United States* (1879).[61]

Third: Wampum and the wampum belt in particular are often overinterpreted as cultural *metaphors* instead of treated as agents of linguistic and economic *transfer,*[62] especially so in works of European and European-style art. One such example is a painting of Hendrick (also known as Taiennoken or Tee Yee Neen Ho Ga Row; plate 10), one of the portraits that Queen Anne commissioned after she received four leaders of the Iroquois Confederacy—"Indian Kings"— at the royal court in 1710. As Benson J. Lossing describes in *Our Country* (1875), Benjamin Franklin was present when Hendrick—accompanied by the chiefs of the Six Nations who gave wampum belts of friendship to delegates at the important assembly gathered in Philadelphia in 1742—gave his famous speech upbraiding the English colonists' strategies in the war against the French.[63]

Indian counsel on how and why to conduct war was much appreciated by the planners of war and their generals.

Countermarking

These five factors—inflation, counterfeiting, debt, diplomacy, and democracy—and then some, taken together, suggest that discomforted anglophones, tender about their own legal tender past, have some warrant (if not also a real want) to believe that European Americans not only destroyed an existing Native American economy (presumably a foregone conclusion) but also transformed it. European Americans of various stripes made the "art and money," that is wampum (and the conditions of counterfeitness, as both representation and exchange, that went along with it), their own official currency. They produced wampum in their factories in such abundance that inflation resulted; and having learned from experiments, they created paper money, and hence both defined and financed a democratic and confederate revolution. One might say they reconstructed wampum in their own image, as if making a "countermark" over it and in it.

In his essay "The Poet" (1844), Ralph Waldo Emerson wrote about "Life, which can dwarf any and every circumstance, and to which the belt of wampum, and the commerce of America, are alike."[64] The countermarks of cultures are "the small types struck on the coin after it had left the mint," as Humphreys writes (1853).[65] The practice of countermarking is part of an imperial and often brutally linguistic conqueror tradition extending back thousands of years, including the Hapsburg and Ottoman Empires and extending almost as far back as Alexander the Great and the parallel bilingual coins of India.[66] One finds countermarks on Greek imperial coins, including the interesting issues from Akragas, and also on Roman imperial coins and on Byzantine coins with Arabic inscriptions.[67] During periods of colonial rebellion in eastern Palestine in the second century B.C., the counterstrikes usually come from the rebel side, as for Simon bar Kochba's coins.[68]

The countermark on a coin is as good as to say, "What's yours is mine," if not also to say, in assimilative, almost cannibalistic fashion, "You are me."[69] An example comes from the Spanish dominions (fig. 93): these "bits"—actually segments—were "Americanized" by means of cutting and counterstamping. Legal tender stemmed from the value of the under-coin, not from the counterstamp.

Such coins indicate neither a bubbling melting pot (of disappearing currencies and languages) nor a colorful mosaic (of mutually tolerant cultures) but rather an imperialist scalping shears that shaves the currency and devalues the national currency. And, by way of example, they help to explain what happened to wampum.

93. Coin. Brazil. Eight reales counter-stamped to 960 reis. 1808–10. John VI Prince Regent is countermarked. ANS 1001.1.2590.

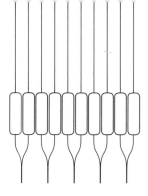

CHAPTER TEN

What Happened to Wampum

KETTOTANESE—LEND ME MONEY.

—WILLIAM WOOD, "A SMALL NOMENCLATOR
OF THE INDIAN LANGUAGE" (1634)

———

THE BUSINESS OF AMERICA IS BUSINESS.

—ATTRIBUTED TO PRESIDENT CALVIN COOLIDGE
SPEAKING TO THE AMERICAN SOCIETY
OF NEWSPAPER EDITORS (1925)

Syncretism

What happened to wampum? For one thing, Americans got much of their practices in the monetary realm from the Indians and then forgot about what they had done. A useful analogy is provided by parallel language experience: the way in which borrowing and lack of acknowledgment go hand in hand in that already corresponding realm. After all, there have been many hundreds of "loan words" from the Native American languages. Not all are associated with economic exchange. Most of these terms are names of places (for example, "Massachusetts"). There are also the terms for various items that were unknown before the American settling by Europeans: animals (e.g., moose), plants (pipsissewa), clothing (moccasins), foods (pemmican), kinds of gods or spirits (the Manitou), new types of geological and waterway formations (sea-purses), novel means of transportation (kayaks), seemingly unusual kinship relations (squaws), and so forth. In the twentieth century, Anglo-Americans—unlike their French- *and* English-speaking neighbors to the north—were systematically (although perhaps unconsciously) ridding themselves of most loan words of Indian origin.[1] A few Indian words, borrowed in the nineteenth century, remain crucial to anthropologists—*totem*, for example, and *potlatch*—who hardly seem able to do without them. The borrowing process works the other way around, too. The Indians borrowed from the Europeans, including many words expressing a certain derogatory quality. *Moonias* probably comes from a pidgin word for *Montréalais*. *Yankee* may come from the Cherokee word *eankke*, meaning "slave" or "coward."[2] Another view is that *yankee* comes from an Indian "corruption" of the English-language word *English*.[3] Canadians, who nowadays use many more words borrowed from Indian languages than modern Americans do, use the verb *to yankee* as a synonym for "to cheat."[4]

We *call* the terms we take from other languages "loan words." The phrase suggests that the borrower has some sort of obligation or intention to pay back what he took. More often than not, however, we forget the loan. We fail to recognize the fact of what some writers have called "glottophagia." (*Glottophagia* refers to the way that one group of people absorbs, or digests, another group's language, or tongue.)[5] For example, Daniel Usner, in his essay "Iroquois Livelihood," asks a rhetorical question about Americans' parallel "forgetting" of where they learned a good part of their agricultural knowledge. "How could a generation of men who has witnessed, even contributed to, the destruction of bountiful Iroquois and Cherokee fields and orchards during the American Revolution fail to recognize the agricultural traditions of eastern North American Indians?"[6] We would do well actually to try to answer the parallel question in the arenas of wampum and language. Most human beings tend to project onto their human creditors (lenders) their own status as debtors (borrowers). In the realm of language borrowing, the Englishman James Gilchrist thus complains in 1824, "The naked savages of Indiana already speak a corrupt English (or Yankee)."[7] Perhaps that observation was accurate regarding the various Indian pidgins. But it also expresses Gilchrist's own awareness, at once fearful and prideful, about the changing status of the "once-pure" "English" language that he himself was now speaking. Would American culture become impure (at best) or savage (at worst)?

Merely *lexical* glottophagia in the linguistic realm (of the sort that Gilchrist attributes to the Indians and fears for the English) is not the central focus of this little book. That focus is the ongoing systemic and *monetary* glottophagia informing the grammar of increasingly cross-cultural monetary systems, including their languages of credit.[8] The syncretism here helps to develop a powerful, possibly unique, "American" system of representation and exchange—and eventually, of production.

Vanishing

By the beginning of the twentieth century, many Americans no longer wanted syncretic Indian culture. Instead, they craved the idea of the "inevitably" vanishing Indian. This craving matched the rise of popular summer camps with Indian names and nostalgic themes. Now whites could safely become Indians. In the numismatic arena, there was parallel controversy about the Augustus Saint-Gaudens ten-dollar piece (1907) (fig. 94). People complained that "[Lady] Liberty [was] shown wearing an Indian headdress instead of the traditional Phrygian Liberty cap."

94. Coin. Philadelphia. Ten dollars. Gold. 1907. Indian Head. Designed by Augustus Saint-Gaudens. ANS 0000.999.4575.

95. Coin. Philadelphia. Five cents. Buffalo Nickel. 1913. Designed by James Earle Fraser, a former assistant to Saint Gaudens. ANS 1913.147.9.

Theodore Roosevelt, who was then President, made the case in favor of the coin: "There is no more reason why a feather headdress should always be held to denote an Indian than why a Phrygian cap should always be held to denote a Phrygian. The Indian in his own way finely symbolizes freedom and a life of liberty . . . and it was eminently fitting that such a head should carry a very beautiful and a purely and characteristically American headdress."[9]

In 1913, under President William Howard Taft, there came the Indian Head nickel (fig. 95). Thanks to this coin's racial stereotyping and its presentation of the noble "brave," many people believed that the coin was "genuinely Indian." The sculptor, James Earle Fraser, had reportedly designed the head from sittings with Iron Tail, Big Tree, and Two Moons.[10] On the other side of this coin, which soon came to be called wampum, was represented that other creature—the free-ranging buffalo—whose supposedly inevitable vanishing had been exacerbated by European Americans' avarice, short-sightedness, and even needless cruelty.

Repatriation

What happened to wampum? How and why were tens of thousands of wampum belts disassembled and lost? To begin with, they were discarded by all sides. The philologist and anthropologist Horatio Hale even points to instances where "the written explanations attached to [the wampum belts] . . . have disappeared."[11] (Hale was a student with Henry David Thoreau at Harvard, where they both heard Emerson deliver his "American Scholar" 1837 commencement address.) From his home in Ontario, near the Six Nations Reserve, Hale recalled in 1896 how easy it was for Indians, including Chief Peter Clarke, to "forget" the aesthetic and economic role of wampum: "In the space of less than two centuries which has elapsed since Indians ceased to manufacture wampum, the knowledge not merely of their forefathers' mode of making it, but of the fact that it was an article of native workmanship, has in some tribes been lost."[12] If a devastated people, traumatized by genocide, famine, and disease, should so forget, why then should not those who benefitted materially and intellectually from the devastation and suffered from variously repressed bad conscience and ill faith not also easily forget what they had learned from wampum and even whence they learned it? And nowadays: How can one remember, after all, what one actually believes he has never known and therefore never forgotten?

Many "original" wampum strings were disassembled and then recycled for purposes presumed better suited to Indians circumstances. In her book *Wampum,* Anne Molloy writes, "When the last official Onondaga Keeper of the Wampum, Abram LaForte, took over the tribe's treasury, it . . . was only twelve belts. By 1878, his people saw no need for an official Keeper. The bag holding the wampum passed from hand to hand. One piece and then another was snipped of beads for religious ceremonies. . . . In time, some tribes in Maine found new uses for wampum [sometimes for betrothal and marriage and sometimes for tourist trinkets]."[13] But not all people forgot wampum or disassembled it to serve other purposes. A few shells and strings came into the possession of museums and various educational and governmental institutions. Some of these items have been repatriated—given back to the descendants of their original creators—during the last couple of decades.[14] Often that repatriation is strictly limited; the Indians of New Brunswick still pray for the return of their wampum belts: *Ktahcuwi-imiyapon weci-apaciptasik wapapihil* (We have to pray for the wampum belts to be returned).

The main question in the present book, however, is not what happened to the original material objects. Rather, the central focus is what happened to the economic and semiotic *system* of wampum and its reception. Some might have it that the wampum economy as such itself also "vanished" long ago. That was already a timeworn theme in 1925, as suggested in the article "What 'Wampum' Was" ["Ce qu'était le 'wampum'"].[15] By the 1920s, in fact, too great an attention to the material of wampum—as beautiful concatenations of shells and beads together with string—served to mask, in the tradition of mascotry,[16] its genuinely financial and spiritual aspect. Value-neutral economics too relegated wampum to the dustbin of history, or seemed to.

Alphabetization

What happened? On the one hand, the wampum belt became a "secular" commodity. Indians began to sell them to European-American "tourists" as something like souvenirs and jewelry beginning in the early nineteenth century. (At around the same time, as Francis Parkman remarks, European wampum-making machines were rendering obsolete the old "wampum beads.")[17] Many of the belts in museums today, the very ones that Indians seek to repatriate, are tourist pieces.

On the other hand, wampum belts were now often "made to order." When they were ordered by the church, they became "religious" sacred objects. Missionaries incorporated wampum belts, woven with various Christian emblems and letterings, into church collections and displays.

96. Drawing. "Religious" wampum belts at the Chapelle de la Lorette of the Mission de Notre-Dame de Lorette near Québec City. From Samuel Douglas Smyth Huyghe's manuscript "Some Accounts of Wampum," 1846. Mx XN1495, Museum Victoria, Melbourne, Australia. Photo courtesy of Museum Victoria.

There are, for example, the lettered wampum belts at the Chapelle de la Lorette of the Mission de Notre-Dame de Lorette in Québec (fig. 96). The mission was mostly for Hurons. Hale writes, "There, at what is known as New Lorette, their descendants remain to this day, a half-caste people, French in complexion, language and religion, but Indians in habits and character, a favorite study of travelers." The chapel and its contents were destroyed by fire in 1862.[18]

There is also the Vatican Wampum Belt (figs. 97 and 98).[19] This belt includes the almost indecipherable self-referential inscription "WHOMPOM." The inscription, along with other insignia, ally the older "autochthonous" medium of exchange (wampum) with the Christian God. The alliance is not far off for a missionary code that regards the love of money as the root of evil and claims God as the highest good. There are many other such "lettered belts," already discussed, from the nineteenth century.[20] Many were (or are) in the numerous wampum collections overseas (fig. 99).

97. Wampum belt. Lake of Two Mountains, Québec. 1831. Vatican Museums, AM-3292.

98. Detail, wampum belt. Lake of Two Mountains, Québec. 1831.
Inscription: WHOMPOM. Vatican Museums, AM-3292.

99. Wampum belt. Date unknown. Musée de l'Homme, Paris. Drawing from a photograph.
Inscription: VIRGIN.IMMAC.HVRD.D. Beauchamp 271.

A few of the lettered wampum belts are secular, and many of these are distinctly bicultural, often also pseudo-bilingual. One example would be the Simcoe Belt from the 1790s (see figure 50). All such wampum merits interpretation along with the *apparently* bilingual Russian-Arabic coins bearing pseudo-scripts—or essentially "illegible" lettering—discussed earlier (see figures 23 and 24). For example, the wampum belt sometimes associated with the marriage of Molly Molasses (fig. 53) bears an apparently roman-alphabet inscription. However, that inscription, like the ones on the dengas we have considered, is pseudo-script. Important to any study of semiotic syncretism, there are many belts that, like the Simcoe Belt, suggest the effects of encounters on both sides, in this case, both Indian and European. These belts point to a medley of bilingual or bicultural writings, hieroglyphs, pictures, and bilingual adaptations, often with commercial and political implications having to do with both credit and trust. Governor William Burnett gave such a belt, lettered "*G R*" (King George), to the Six Nations in Albany in 1724. In 1756, Governor William Denny of Pennsylvania, seeking to ratify an important treaty, "gave a very large belt with the figures of three men in it, representing His Majesty King George taking hold of the 5 Nations King with one hand, and Teedyuscung the Delaware King with the other, and marked with the following letters and figure: '*G. R.*' [or King George,] '*5 N*' [Five Nations], and '*D. K.*' [Delaware King]."[21]

Wampum—whether or not inscribed (woven) with such roman lettering—became an object of contemplation for European Americans, who soon romanticized the literal (textual) significance. Consider the work of the popular Canadian Métis anglophone poet Emily Pauline Johnson. Johnson adopted the Mohawk name Tekahionwake (meaning "Double Wampum"). Her first book, *The White Wampum* (1895), encourages forgetting the ongoing, systemic financial glottophagia at work in North America. In her poem "Ojistoh," Johnson tells how, after the Hurons capture a Mohawk chief, they invite his wife, Ojistoh, to become queen of the Hurons in order further to humiliate the Mohawks. Ojistoh's response is angry:

> O! evil, evil face of them they sent
> With evil Huron speech: "Would I consent
> To take of wealth? Be queen of all their tribe?
> Have wampum ermine?"[22]

The same conflict between Indian and European wealth informs Eleanor Leprohon's poem "The White Maiden and the Indian Girl" (1881). The girl prefers her "rich wampum belts" to the civilized white's "diamonds of price untold."[23] When translators turned Leprohon's writings to French, her works became popular among the French-speaking tribes in Québec.

Knowing Who's Who

HERE IS WAMPUM.
GIVE ME BRANDY FOR IT.
FARMER: WHAT IS WAMPUM?
WHAT SHALL I DO WITH IT?

——AUGUSTUS VAN BUREN

Many people have said that the Indian attitude toward money is naïve—all the more especially so when it comes to paper money, which some Indians call "frog-skin," according to Webster's dictionary. The Sioux writer John Lame Deer writes, "The Green Frog Skin—that's what I call a dollar bill. In our [the American Indians'] attitude toward [a dollar bill] lies the biggest difference between Indians and whites."[24]

Recall Lame Deer's version of a well-known Indian story about Chief Little Dog, an Algonquian-speaking member of the American Blackfeet. In 1850, Little Dog massacred a wagon train and plundered the wagons. He failed to bring home a box of coins, however, because he thought them to be merely "buttons without eyes."[25] Lame Deer praises the chief's innocence of money along with his "higher" intuitions about exchange. At the same time, Lame Deer denies the European Americans the sociopathology of money that they themselves eschew; that is to say, he assumes that European Americans do not play around with money and do not have their own ceremonies with relevant counterparts to coup stick and wampum.

Lame Deer is hardly alone in presuming that Native Americans did not understand European money. In *Wampum, War, and Trade Goods,* Hagerty recalls an incident in seventeenth-century New Netherland whose retelling suggests the same prejudice. In Hagerty's version of the story, Dominie Johannes Megapolensis is trying to explain to an Indian chief the value of a rijkdealder. "The chief laughed, saying, 'You are fools to value a piece of iron so highly.'" Hagerty claims the story shows that the chief did not understand the value of European currency. "The Indians thought of [money, says Hagerty,] as being of no more value than any piece of metal. They had not yet grasped the idea of letting a surrogate substitute for goods in transaction. Coins were an abstraction in this sense. Where trade was the issue, the Mohawk trader lived close to reality and things passed for what they were with him. A beaver or a kettle or blanket had a value he could readily comprehend."[26]

Hagerty probably sells the chief short. Maybe the chief's laughter indicates that he recognized, in European coinage, something of the idiosyncratic peculiarities of the Indians' own systems of exchange. Maybe the chief sees the humorous absurdity of the Dutch interlocutor's preferring rijkdealder to wampum at a time when wampum was legal tender according to the government of New Netherland. Certainly, Hagerty's notion that "a beaver . . . had a value [the Indian] could readily comprehend" is a strange and telling misprision of most Indian systems of representation and exchange. Hagerty is correct that a *beaver* "was" a beaver. (How *could* that be "wrong"?) At some times, though, for the Indians, a beaver might "be" a beaver *pelt.* Or it might "be" a diminutive copper *sculpture* of a beaver.[27] After all, seventeenth-century Dutchmen well knew that wampum was the basis of the beaver trade as well as the other way around. When Peter Stuyvesant argued against the Dutch East India Company's view that wampum should be "reduced to a silver base," he put forth that "Wampum is the source and the mother of the beaver trade, and for goods only, without wampum, we cannot obtain beavers from the savages."[28] It is small wonder that Canadians still depict beavers on the numismatic sculptures that are their nickels (five-cent coins) and that Oregonians minted their "beaver coins" in 1849. In *Indian Money as a Factor in New England Civilization* (1884), William Weeden wrote that wampum is the magnet which drew the beaver out of the interior forests." Weeden may as well have had in mind the magnetic, bilingual tetradrachms minted by Vima Kadphises.[29]

Some anthropologists err in much the same way as Hagerty does when they argue that wampum was not Indian money because wampum was often ornamental and money cannot be ornamental. It is true that much wampum was also "ornamental."[30] But genuinely monetary tokens are "used" as ornament in many cultures—as shown in my book *Art and Money.* An argument that ornament cannot be money suggests a misunderstanding of what money is that guarantees from the start a certain misprision of how wampum functions.

In fact, most Indian groups were remarkably adept at understanding the European's money and law. James Fenimore Cooper caught on to this fact in his *Last of the Mohicans:*

"Magua is a red-skin; he wants not the beads of the pale-faces."

"Gold, silver, powder, lead—all that a warrior needs shall be in thy wigwam; all that becomes the greatest chief."[31]

There is plenty of evidence that Indians traded with coins, and even banked by means of them, soon after early contacts with Europeans.[32] During the first centuries of linguistic and economic encounter, Indian methods of exchange influenced the Europeans much more than has yet been acknowledged. Nicolas Benjamin Doucet had remarked on this, and on its reverse, in his work on tariff law (Montréal, 1840). At that time, the First Peoples of Upper Canada wanted to import shells from the United States in order to carry on regular trade with other groups, including both Anglo- and French Canadians. Doucet's work focused on the "fundamental principles of the laws of Canada, as they existed under the natives, as they were changed under the French kings, and as they were modified and altered under the domination of England."[33]

Skill in the monetary sphere is suggested by commercial "texts" written by Native Americans who had learned to use the roman alphabet. In 1709, for example, the Wampanoag woman Patte Epheum (Betty Ephraim) wrote the following in a partly pidginized, Algonquian-Massachusett language (fig. 100).

nen—patte epheum mache unnumau mone peter mussauwowaud 55 Ser—wutche matt[.m] doonk wutche wechoo wuttotoonk nessinnechag kah wutche pasuk connon wonoh.

[I, Patte Epheum, have given money to Peter Mussauwowaud, 55 [?] shillings [?], for the bargain for the house [and] his property, twenty, for one common.][34]

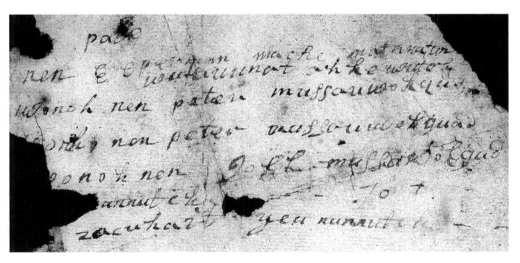

100. Detail, legal paper written by Patte Epheum (Betty Ephraim). Nantucket. July 17, 1709. Massachusetts Historical Society, Boston (Misc., Unbound).

Epheum even uses the English-language *mone* [money] instead of the Massachusett-derived term *wampum*. *Mone* here is not a naïve translation of, or synonym for, wampum. By this time, wampum had already gone out of use as a foreign/native *legal* tender in Massachusetts.

The Last Laugh

There is a small trompe l'oeil painting, *Old King George; or, The Last Laugh* (1930s), by the German-American artist and money counterfeiter Otis Kaye. The work includes a near-perfect replica of the only issue of American paper money with an Indian for the central motif, a five-dollar banknote (plate 17).

For the actual five-dollar silver certificate, designers—including the engraver George F. C. Smillie—had commemorated one of the Hunkpapa Sioux who "counted coup" at the Battle of Little Big Horn (1876). Kaye's own painting (1951) of that battle gives prominence to "scalping" even as it draws attention to the shell hair pipes—tubular shells—that the Sioux used both for making military breastplates and as instruments of trade (plate 18).

The use of hair pipes—similar to that of wampum—predates the first arrival of white traders and was important to many of the tribes I have discussed in this book, including the Delaware, Ojibwa, and Seneca.[35] At one time, the term *hair pipe* was common; European and British traders often refer to hair pipes, and the most American important diplomats, including George Morgan, likewise use the term in their writings. ("The origin of the name [*hair pipe*] is obscure," as Ewers writes, but that hardly explains why comprehensive English-language dictionaries fail even to record the term.)[36]

In *Old King George,* which recalls the "counterfeit" aspect of state-supported wampum as well as other anachronistic media, the artist indicates his own name, *Otis Kaye,* by means of the acronym *OK* near the Joker playing card: the nail head represents *O* and the first letter of the King of Clubs playing card presents the *K*. In other such trompe l'oeil artworks—including the large painting *Land of the Free, Home of the Brave*—Otis Kaye signs his painted "counterfeit" paper money as "Otis Kaye."

It is as if OK were not only the artist (who makes the painting) but also the American secretary of the treasury (who makes the money). This is the same epigraphic tradition in which worked Thomas Nast ("This is Money by Act of the Congress" and "This is a Cow by the Act of the Artist") and René Magritte ("This is Not a Pipe"). Ever the Joker ("O! 'tis Kaye!"), *Kaye* locates his work in the tradition of those German Americans who, like Whorf and Sapir, helped to found a sober, linguistically informed study of Indian languages and exchange practices. In fact, the "English" term *OK* or *Okay*—which moniker Otis Kaye adopts as his own—probably comes from the Choctaws' Mobilian trading language, indicating assent.[37] Wampum is its conchological counterpart. That *OK* is now the most widely used word among all the world's languages suggests its draw on the global scale.[38]

The trompe l'oeil newspaper clipping in Otis Kaye's *Old King George* (fig. 101) recalls that OK, or the *O*ld *K*ing (George)—the initials are reversed from the lettered wampum belt that

101. Detail, *Old King George; or, The Last Laugh.*
Painting by Otis Kaye, 1930s. CS.

Burnett gave to the Six Nations (1724)—was supposed to "okay" all paper monies but he never did and now he never will. OK (King George), having lost his American colonies, suggests that his erstwhile subjects have become, in the wake of their independence, the very savages, with their wampum and worthless paper, that they themselves condemned. (Conrad Weiser had already said, during the colonial wars leading up to the American Revolution, that all Americans had to do was "get Wampum to do the business.")[39] OK (Otis Kaye) as artist, now speaking for himself, remarks with some irony that the banks have the last laugh. The newspaper reads, "Old King George joked, 'Americans are worthless savages.' But BanKs [*sic*] today have the last laugh said Otis Kaye." Wampum won out. Governor William Bradford, writing *Of Plymouth Foundation* (1630s-40s), was right in his prediction: wampum, transformed, proved itself to be America's most powerful drug of choice.[40] The fear or hope, expressed willy-nilly by America's long-standing Indian mascotry, was also America's reality.

Roanoke, and How

"WHAT SEEK YOU, MY WILD FLOWER,"
SAID THE GENERAL
[GEORGE WASHINGTON AT WEST POINT IN 1782].
[THE INDIAN GIRL] STARTED TO HER FEET, DREW
A SMALL TOMAHAWK FROM HER BELT OF WAMPUM,
AND IMITATED THE ACT OF SCALPING THE ENEMY;
THEN AGAIN WAVING HER HAND AS FORBIDDING
HIM TO ADVANCE, SHE DARTED INTO THE BUSHES,
LEAVING HIM LOST IN AMAZEMENT.

——HENRY C. WATSON

In the end, wampum is lost to us, or so we say. But *how?* Perhaps in the way that the colony of Roanoke (1585–87), in the Outer Banks of North Carolina, is lost to us. That its name, *Roanoke,* means "wampum" is not surprising. The right kind of shell is in the geographic area—people there had used it as wampum since pre-Columbian times—and various tribes there were known as the region's wampum bankers.[41]

"America's first founders" is what the settlers at Roanoke are called.[42] Their colony's historiography began auspiciously with Thomas Hariot's *Briefe and True Report of the New Found Land of Virginia.*[43] This work was published in 1588, the same year that the Spanish Armada went down and Shakespeare wrote his first play. Thanks to John White's illustrations for the *Report,* many scholars say that the Roanoke Colony gave Europeans their "first pictures of America."[44] Despite all that, and more, Roanoke soon became "The Lost Colony" or the "Abandoned Colony."[45] What happened to Roanoke?

The question is one of those so-called mysteries, riddles, or enigmas that make for national literature, ranging from George Chapman, Ben Jonson, and John Marston's *Eastvvard Hoe* (1605) in England to Paul Green's "symphonic drama" *The Lost Colony* (1939) in the United States.[46] Moreover, all sorts of academic, archeological, or aesthetic studies aim to discover "the true Roanoke" and explain what happened to it.[47] According to one convincing account, the Roanoke settlers were "absorbed" or "assimilated" by the local Lumbee or Croatan Indians. The settlers learned to dance with the Indians and joined in with their ways of speech and trade.[48] Lew Barton calls this version of what happened to Roanoke "the most ironic story in American history":[49] America's first founders—"We the People"—turn out to become Indian braves.

Later on too, as we have seen, the settlers found Indian ways in the brave New World both attractive and needful as well as strangely familiar. In his *Generall Historie of Virginia* (1624), written about the Jamestown Settlement, Captain John Smith reminds us that roanoke, or wampum, occasioned "as much dissention among the Salvages, as gold and silver amongst Christians." Governor William Bradford, of *Mayflower* fame, warned in *Of Plymouth Plantation* (1620–47) that wampum would become the British settlers' drug of choice. So the path from wampum to Wall Street was laid out from the beginning.[50] And how.

George and Ira Gershwin put forth the phrase *and how!* in the lyrics of a song-and-dance routine that they wrote for Ginger Rogers and Fred Astaire:

> They laughed at us *and how!*
> But Ho, Ho, Ho!
> Who's got the last laugh now?[51]

How is "an [emphatic] exclamation to attract attention." English etymologists claim that the term is more or less universal among all human beings: a "natural utterance."[52] The Russian-Jewish Gershwin brothers knew better. They understood that, in the hyphenated culture of anglophone America, this particular use of *how* also derives from such Algonquian usages as *hau* (in the Omaha language), *haau* (in the Huron), and *háo* (in the Sioux).[53] The variants of *how* range otherwise from *hugh* in James Fenimore Cooper's pity-inspiring *Last of the Mohicans* (1826) to "ugh, ugh, ugh" in Howard Hawks's parodic movie *Monkey Business* (1952). The Gershwin brothers' "Ho, Ho, Ho" in *Shall We Dance* (1937) mimics the triplicate Santee Sioux *ho* that Charles Alexander Eastman preferred for his memoir *Indian Boyhood* (1902): "When the preliminaries had been completed, our leader sounded the big drum and we all said 'A-ho-ho-ho!' as a sort of amen. Then the choir began their song and whenever they ended a verse, we all said again 'A-ho-ho-ho!' At last they struck up the chorus and we all got upon our feet and began to dance, by simply lifting up one foot and then the other, with a slight swing to the body."[54] Eastman, whose birth name was "Pitiful Last" (*hadakah*), had been a medical doctor at Wounded Knee (1890), where American troops had gone to quell the Indian "Ghost Dance Movement."[55] Once there, the machine gunners put a brutal end to the centuries-long war dance.

Ambivalent laughter—*ho ho ho*—has helped twenty-first-century historians of money get around the study of wampum even as wampum has informed American economic development.

In the end, though, the trompe l'oeil newspaper clipping in Otis Kaye's painting *The Last Laugh* has it right: "Old King George joked, 'Americans are worthless savages.'" American banks had the last laugh.

Early on, American bankers and printers adapted the institutions of wampum and made it legal tender. In the colonies, during the period leading up to the American Revolution, paper money gave the colonists a real control over their own affairs. From 1690 until 1900, this "Indian and white ingenuity," as John Ewers had it, was documented on the very face of national currency and in the grammar of its banking system. So the paper money that Kaye depicts in *Home of the Brave* is only the beginning. Between the Boston Tea Party, when the colonists dressed as Mohawks, and Willie Wampum, whose football fans whooped like Indians, America has come into its own.[56]

NOTES

Introduction

The epigraph is from Ralph Waldo Emerson, "The Poet," in *Essays: Second Series* (1844), reprinted in *Essays and English Traits* (New York: P. F. Collier, 1909), 176.

1. On "sale" terminologies elsewhere, and where the language issue is quite different, see Marshall Joseph Becker, "Lenape Land Sales, Treaties, and Wampum Belts," *Pennsylvania Magazine of History of Biography* 103.8 (July 1984): 351–56; and Marc Shell, "The Ring of Gyges," in Shell, *The Economy of Literature* (Baltimore: Johns Hopkins University Press, 1978), 11–62.

2. The quoted phrase is from John C. Ewers, "Hair Pipes in Plains Indian Adornment: A Study in Indian and White Ingenuity," Anthropological Paper 50, *Bureau of American Ethnology Bulletin* 164 (Washington, D.C: Government Printing Office, 1957), 29–85, plates 13–37.

3. Elizabeth S. Peña, "Wampum Production in New Netherland and Colonial New York: The Historical and Archeological Context" (Ph.D. diss., Boston University, 1990), 44. See also her "Wampum Production in New Netherland and Colonial New York," *Bead Forum* 17 (1990): 8–14. Citations below refer to the dissertation.

4. See William A. Turnbaugh, *The Material Culture of RI-1000: A Mid-Seventeenth Century Narragansett Burial Site in North Kingstown, Rhode Island* (Kingston: Department of Sociology and Anthropology, University of Rhode Island, 1984).

5. *Oxford English Dictionary* (hereafter, *OED*), s.v. "wampum."

6. William Babcock Weeden, *Indian Money as a Factor in New England Civilization* (Baltimore: Johns Hopkins University, 1884). The Johns Hopkins University Press, the first such press in the United States, was founded in 1878. Weeden is also author of the informative two-volume book *Economic and Social History of New England 1620–1789* (Boston: Houghton, Mifflin, 1894).

7. See Alexander Del Mar, *The History of Money in America from the Earliest Times to the Establishment of the Constitution* (New York: Cambridge Encyclopedia Co., 1899).

8. The phrase *pay through the nose* means "to pay excessively"; it is synonymous with some uses of the verb "to bleed or to be bled." *OED*, s.v. "nose" III.11. One view about its etymology is that that the phrase comes from the Danish custom of slitting the noses of those who did not pay the Danegeld in Ireland. Glyn Davies, *A History of Money from Ancient Times to the Present Day* (Cardiff: University of Wales Press, 2002), 39.

9. For Peter Minuit, see *Documents from the Dutch West India Company: Samuel Sidwell Randall's History of the State of New York, for the Use of Common Schools, Academies, Normal and High Schools, and Other Seminaries of Instruction* (New York: J. B. Ford, 1870). This volume is among the first to claim that the

purchase was in a medium other than coin. For the stories about wampum beads and the like, see Francis Peter Jr., "The Beads That Did Not Buy Manhattan Island," in *One Man's Trash Is Another Man's Treasure*, ed. Alexandra van Dongen (Rotterdam: Museum Boymansvan Beuningen, 1996), 53–70.

10. William O. Taylor, *With Custer on the Little Bighorn: A Newly Discovered First-Person Account,* foreword by Greg Martin (New York: Viking, 1996), 159. See also General George Crook, *His Autobiography* (Norman: University of Oklahoma Press, 1946).

11. Harold Bherer, Sylvie Gagnon, and Jacinte Roberge, *Wampum and Letters Patent: Exploratory Study of Native Entrepreneurship* (Halifax, Nova Scotia: Institute of Research on Public Policy, 1990), 219. The authors remark, "It is not that far from wampum to letters patent. . . . The very existence of such artifacts among the natives signifies that a certain formalization of relations and exchanges as was foreign to their culture, even before the arrival of the White man."

12. See George R. Price, "Wampumpeag: The Impact of the 17th Century Wampum Trade on Native Cultures in Southern New England and New Netherlands," (master's thesis, University of Montana, Missoula, 1996).

13. See Marc Bloch, *Esquisse d'une histoire monétaire de l'Europe* (Paris: A. Colin, 1954). The sketch was published some years after Bloch was killed by the Nazis.

Chapter 1: Money and Language

The epigraph is from Alexander Del Mar, *Ancient Britain in the Light of Modern Archeological Discoveries* (New York: Cambridge Encyclopedia Co., 1896), 178.

1. Aphra Behn, *The Rover; or, The Banished Cavaliers,* in *Plays, written by the late ingenious Mrs. Behn,* 3rd ed. (London: Printed for Mary Poulson and sold by A. Bettesworth and F. Clay, 1724), part 2, act 3.

2. Gilbert Parker, *Mrs. Falchion: A Novel* (London: Methuen, 1893), 118. For a relevant (and contemporary) treatment of the Chinook Jargon, see George Shaw, *The Chinook Jargon and How to Use It: A Complete and Exhaustive Lexicon of the Oldest Trade Language of the American Continent* (Seattle: Rainer Printing Company, 1909). For the counterpart Choctaw trading language, see my book *The Painting in the Trash Bin,* forthcoming from the University of Chicago Press. No consensus has been reached as to how wampum was worn. What we call a "wampum belt" the French call a "collar of wampum."

3. John Stuart Mill, *Principles of Political Economy,* 5th London ed. (New York: D. Appleton, 1865), bk. 3, ch. 20: "Of the Foreign Exchanges" (2:176). See also Benjamin J. Cohen, *The Geography of Money* (Ithaca: Cornell University Press, 1998), 35.

4. Horatio Hale, "Four Huron Wampum Records: A Study of Aboriginal American History. History of Mnemonic Symbols," *Journal of the Royal Anthropological Institute of Great Britain and Ireland* 26 (1897): 229; See also Hale, "Indian Migrations as Evidenced by Language," *American Antiquaries* (1883): 18–28, 108–24.

5. *Nummicide* is my "linguistic coinage," from the Latin *nummus,* "coin," and *caedere,* "kill."

6. Ellen Hoffman, "One World, One Currency," *Omni* June 1991, 51.

7. Fred Hirsch, *Money International* (London: Penguin, 1967), 20.

8. Cohen, *Geography of Money,* 4.

9. Michael Mussa, "One Money for How Many?" in *Understanding Interdependence: The Macroeconomics of the Open Economy*, ed. Peter B. Kenan (Princeton: Princeton University Press, 1995), 98. See also Mussa,

"Macroeconomic Policy Implications of Currency Zones," in *Policy Implications of Trade and Currency Zones: A Symposium Sponsored by the Federal Reserve Bank of Kansas City, Jackson Hole, Wyoming, August 22–24, 1991* (Kansas City, Mo.: Federal Reserve Bank of Kansas City, 1991), 213–19. Mussa also emphasizes that "there are few examples of national governments that have not sought to enforce a single monetary standard within their domain of political authority" (quoted in Cohen, *Geography of Money*, 27).

10. Stanley Fischer, "Seigniorage and the Case for National Money," *Journal of Political Economy* 90.2 (April 1982): 298.

11. Pascal Salin, "General Introduction," *Currency Competition and Monetary Union*, ed. Pascal Salin (The Hague. Martinus Nijhoof, 1984), 1–26 (quotation, 3).

12. Herman Harmelink, letter to the *New York Times,* January 12, 1972, 38.

13. Richard O'Brien, *Global Financial Integration: The End of Geography* (New York: Council on Foreign Relations, 1992).

14. Cohen, *Geography of Money,* 120 ("de-territorialized"); Eric Helleiner, "Historicizing Territorial Currencies: Monetary Structures, Sovereignty, and the Nation-State," paper presented at the 1996 Annual Meeting of the International Studies Association, 19 ("promote a different sense"); Helleiner adds, "The tendency of universalism to veer towards imperialist tyranny should be taken in to account" (ibid.). Cohen (*Geography of Money,* 92) suggests as much when he quotes from Arthur Jensen's speech to Howard Beale in the 1976 movie *Network:* "You are an old man who thinks in terms of nations and peoples. There are no nations, no peoples, there are no Russians, there are no Arabs, there are no Third Worlds, there is no West. There is only one holistic system of systems, one vast and immense interwoven, interacting, multivariate, multinational dominion of dollars, petro-dollars, electro-dollars, multi-dollars, Reichsmarks, rubles, pounds, and shekels. It is the international system of currency which determines the totality of life on this planet. That is the natural order of things today. That is the atomic, and subatomic, and galactic structure of things today."

15. See Alexander Del Mar, "The Sacred Character of Gold," in Del Mar, *The History of Monetary Systems* (Chicago: C. H. Kerr, 1869), 66–93.

16. Cohen, *Geography of Money,* 39.

17. Marie Therese Boyer-Xambeu, Ghislain Deleplace, and Lucien Gillard, *Private Money and Public Currencies: The 16th Century Challenge,* trans. Azizeh Azodi, foreword by Charles P. Kindleberger (Armonk, N.Y.: M. E. Sharpe, 1994), 105.

18. For use of the term *pegging,* see Cohen, *Geography of Money,* 57. Cohen seems to imagine that, until the nineteenth century, the United States did not distinguish between foreign coins that circulated by law as tender and those that did not (33–34). See also Tomasso Padoa-Schioppa, "The European Monetary System: A Long-Term View," in *The European Monetary System,* ed. Francesco Giavazzi, Stefano Micossi, and Marcus Miller (New York: Cambridge University Press, 1988), ch. 12.

19. For this definition see Henry Alexander (the elder), *Travels and Adventures in Canada and the Indian Territories between the Years 1760 and 1776* (New York: I. Riley, 1809), 305.

20. John George Hodgins, *A History of Canada and the Other British Provinces* (Montréal: John Lovell, 1866), 101.

21. See Laurence Oliphant, *Episodes in a Life of Adventure; or, Moss from a Rolling Stone* (Edinburgh: W. Blackwood, 1887), 72.

22. *Encyclopaedia Britannica* (1888), s.v. "taboo" (by J. G. Frazer), 23:467, col. 1.

23. Shakespeare, *Merchant of Venice,* 4.1. See also Marc Shell, "Language Wars," *CR: The New Centennial Review* 1.2 (2001): 1–17.

24. Paul Samuelson, correspondence with author, July 29, 1997.

25. Del Mar, *Ancient Britain,* 178.

Chapter 2: Foreign Legal Tender

The epigraph is from Thomas Jefferson, *Coinage Report* (April 1790), in *The Writings of Thomas Jefferson,* ed. Henry A. Washington, 9 vols. (Washington, D.C.: Taylor and Maury, 1853–54), 7:173.

1. For Henry James, see Beverley Haviland, "The Return of the Alien: Henry James in New York, 1904," *Henry James Review* 16.3 (1995): 257–63. Tender is defined as "an offer of money, or the like, in discharge of a debt or liability, esp. an offer which thus fulfils the terms of the law and of the liability" (*OED,* s.v. "tender"). Judicially it was held that foreign coins with legal tender status were as much a part of the United States monetary system as domestic coinage, both being rendered current by the statute. See Oscar G. Schilke and Solomon Schilke, *America's Foreign Coins: An Illustrated Standard Catalogue With Valuations of Foreign Coins with Legal Tender Status in the United States, 1793–1857* (New York: Coin and Currency Institute, 1964), 33.

2. On this topic generally, see Charles G. Altz, *Foreign Coins Struck at United States Mints* (Racine, Wisc.: Whitman, 1965).

3. In 1789 Jefferson argued, "Coinage is peculiarly an Attribute of Sovereignty. To transfer its exercise to another Country, is to submit it to another sovereign." He claimed (incorrectly) that "the carrying on a Coinage in a foreign country, as far as the Secretary knows, is without example." In *The Writings of Thomas Jefferson,* ed. Albert Ellery Bergh, 20 vols. (Washington, D.C.: Thomas Jefferson Memorial Association, 1903–4), 3:13, 14.

4. Relevant texts include: *Letter from the Secretary of the Treasury, transmitting a report of the director of the Mint, containing the result of the assays of foreign gold and silver coins* (Washington: Roger Chew Weightman, 1812); *Letter from the Secretary of the Treasury, transmitting a report of the Director of the Mint, of the result of several assays at that establishment, on the gold and silver coins of foreign nations* (Washington: E. De Krafft, 1818); *Letter from the Secretary of the Treasury transmitting a report prepared in obedience to the act: entitled an Act Regulating the Currency of Foreign Coins in the United States, passed April tenth, 1806* (Washington: A. and G. Way, 1809); *Report of the committee [Congress / House], appointed on the twenty-fourth ultimo, to enquire whether any, and what alterations are necessary in the law, intituled "An act regulating foreign coins; and for other purposes"* (Philadelphia: William Ross[?], 1797); *Report of the committee [Congress / House], appointed . . . to inquire into the expediency of amending the laws which regulate the coins of the United States, and foreign coins: accompanied with A Bill Supplementary* (Washington: n.p., 1819]; *Mr. Anderson, from the committee [Congress / House] to whom was referred the bill . . . to repeal so much of the act entitled An Act Regulating Foreign Coins* (Washington: n.p., 1806); *Letter from the Secretary of the Treasury, in obedience to a resolution of the Senate, to inquire into the expediency of continuing in force the act of the 29th of April, 1816: regulating the currency of certain . . .* (Washington: E. De Krafft, 1819).

5. Colonial Hong Kong in 1911 is one example. The 1911 edition of *Encyclopedia Britannica* reports: "The only legal tender is the Mexican dollar, and the British and Hong-Kong dollar, or other silver dollars of equivalent value duly authorized by the governor" (13:659, col. 1).

6. The medio is an obsolete Mexican coin, also used in Cuba. The term *joe* was applied in the southern states of North America, in the West Indies, and elsewhere, to small silver coins forming fractions of the Spanish dollar, or (when these are obsolete) to their value in current money. Now the term is usually applied in the United States to a unit of value equivalent to an eighth of a dollar; used only in even multiples, as four bits, six bits. *OED,* s.v. "bit." See Jefferson, *Autobiography,* in *Writings of Thomas Jefferson*, ed. Washington, vol. 1, appendix, note F ("Notes on the Establishment of a Monetary Unit"), 243–44: "The tenth [of the dollar] will be precisely the Spanish bit, or half-pistareen."

7. The shilling is also called *shiloing*.

8. Just before 1776, for example, there were Dutch *rijksdollars*. Some have argued that this was America's first dollar; see William Justin DeLeonardis, "America's First Dollar?" *The Numismatist* 100.10 (Oct. 1987): 2118–20. Some scholars have noted that the dollar mark has the general form of the familiar "8" of Spanish currency—which was trusted—except that the 8 supposedly became an S, just as two lines distinguish it from the peso.

9. Jerry Martien, *Shell Game: A True Account of Beads and Money in North America,* foreword by Gary Snyder (San Francisco: Mercury House, 1996), 25. Martien documents this claim by citing Harold Wentworth and Stuart Berg Flexner, *Dictionary of American Slang* (New York: Crowell, 1960), where a passage from John O'Hara's *Pal Joey* attests this usage.

10. *AFC,* 42 (circulation amounts), 186 (table showing reis value).

11. Donald H. Kagin, *Private Gold Coins and Patterns of the United States* (New York: Arco, 1981), 2.

12. See Marc Shell, "The Gold Bug," in my *Money, Language, and Thought* (Berkeley: University of California Press, 1982), 5–23.

13. On private coinage, see Kagin, *Private Gold Coins.* Hard times tokens are the subject of Russell Rulau, *Hard Times Tokens, 1832–1844,* 4th ed. (Iola, Wisc.: Krause Publications, 1992), a revised, enlarged edition of Lyman H. Low's 1899 work. See also *Price Catalogue of United States Hard Times Tokens* (Chicago: Hewitt Brothers Numismatic Publications, n.d.).

14. Marjorie K. Akin, "Noncurrency Functions of Chinese Coin," *Historical Archeology* 26.2 (1992): 58–65, includes the viewpoints of those scholars who argued that the wen had a currency function. Many such wen were recovered from the site of Yema-po, an 1870s work camp inhabited by Chinese laborers in the San Francisco Bay area, and they are typical of the coins that were in circulation in China during the period of Chinese immigration to America; most of these wen date to the period of the Ch'ing (Manchu) Dynasty (1662–1850) and were of low monetary value (perhaps one-tenth of an American cent). Wen found in nineteenth-century overseas Chinese settlements often have issue dates preceding the site occupation by one or two centuries. See George R. Miller, Lyssa Stapleton, Martha Barnes, and Sabina Morganti, "The Coins and Gambling Tokens," in *Yema-po: The Overseas Chinese and the Construction of the San Leandro Dam,* ed. George R. Miller, C. E. Smith Occasional Papers in Anthropology no. 2 (East Bay: C. E. Smith Museum of Anthropology, California State University at East Bay 1998). Yema-po, a site designated CA-Ala-423H, is located in the San Francisco Bay area.

15. One such dominion, Florida, became part of the United States in 1819; see the map by Aaron Arrowsmith, *Spanish Dominions in North America,* published in Boston by Thomas and Andrews, 1812.

16. Samuel Manning Welch, *Recollections of Buffalo during the Decade from 1830–1840* (Buffalo: Peter, Paul, and Bro., 1890), 168.

17. "The elimination of this coinage from the monetary system, despite some lingering on because of specie problems after 1857, signalled the demise of foreign elements in the national money." *AFC* 64.

18. Shell, *Economy of Literature,* 83–84. For "Indian hating," see Herman Melville, *The Confidence-Man* (1857), ch. 26: "Containing the metaphysics of Indian-hating." For "Archimedean power," see ibid., ch. 7: "But the main point is the Archimedean money-power that would be brought to bear."

Chapter 3: Translation and Conversion

The epigraph is from Roger Williams, *Key into the Language of America* (London: Gregory Dexter, 1643), 144.

1. See Norman Davis and Colin M. Kraay, *The Hellenistic Kingdoms: Portrait Coins and History* (London: Thames and Hudson, 1973), 238–39.

2. In 1838, the deciphering of the edicts (in Karoshti script) of Emperor Asoka by the archeologist James Prinsep helped to clarify the then obscure history of India and Buddhism; see Prinsep, *Essays on Indian Antiquities, Historic, Numismatic, and Palæographic,* ed. Edward Thomas, 3 vols. (London: J. Murray, 1858). For Champollion, see his *Précis du système hiéroglyphique des anciens Égyptiens, ou Recherches sur les élémens premiers de cette écriture sacrée, sur leurs diverses combinaisons, et sur les rapports de ce système avec les autres méthodes graphiques égyptiennes* (Paris: Treuttel et Würtz, 1824).

3. Consider the *apparently* bilingual coins of India itself, especially those of the Prakit-speaking kings ruling the Deccan (200 B.C. to A.D. 250); see R. Panulerselvam, "Further Light on the Bilingual Coin of the Satavahanas," *Indo-Iranian Journal* 11 (1969): 281.

4. Werner Wycichl, "Al-Andalus (sobre la historia de un nombre)," *Al-Andalus* 17 (1952): 449–50; Joaquín Vallvé, "Sobre algunos problemas de la invasión musulmana," *Anuario de Estudios Medievales* 4 (1967): 361–63.

5. See Y. T. Nercessian, *Attribution and Dating of Armenian Bilingual Trams* (Los Angeles: Armenian Numismatic Society, 1983).

6. Most bilingual dengas, including those with blundered or pseudo-Arabic legends, were struck in the principalities in the East. In Serpukhov, dengas citing Toqtamish were struck under Vladimir Andreevich (1358–1410) and Semyon Vladimirovich (1410–26). In the principality of Dmitrov, dengas with blundered/crude Arabic legends were struck under Peter Dmitrievich (1389–1428). In the principality of Suzdal/Nizhnii Novgorod, Vasilii Dmitrievich Kirdyapa (1387–91), prince of Nizhnii Novgorod, struck dengas citing Toqtamish. On coins from these regions, see Eric R. Schena, "Influence of Islamic and Tatar Coins on the Russian Monetary System," http://s155239215.onlinehome.us/turkic/btn_Cins/Russian_Monetary_systemEn.htm, accessed May 25, 2011.

7. On Caffa, see works of Konstantin Khromov, including his Web page http://www.hordecoins.folgat.net, accessed May 25, 2011. See also Giuseppe Lunardi, *Le monete delle colonie Genovesi* (Genoa: nella sede della Società ligure di storia patria, 1980).

8. Even so, perhaps "Frères" translates as "Brothers" and "Nlle" translates as "N."

9. *OED,* s.v. "bread."

10. This bill is in the Collection Selechonek.

11. David Ames Wells, *Robinson Crusoe's Money; or, The Remarkable Financial Fortunes and Misfortunes of a Remote Island Community,* illus. Thomas Nast (New York: Harper, 1876), 97.

12. A *mondegreen* (or *mondagreen*) is "the mishearing (usually accidental) of a phrase, such that it

acquires a new meaning." Sylvia Wright, "The Death of Lady Mondegreen," *Harper's Magazine,* November 1954, 48–51. For examples, see Gavin Edwards, *When a Man Loves a Walnut* (Old Tappan, N.J.: Fireside, 1997).

13. On false friends see Goeff Parkes and Alan Cornell, *NTC's Dictionary of German False Cognates* (Lincolnwood, Ill.: National Textbook Company Publishing Group, 1992).

14. For another etymology, see Eric Partridge, *A Dictionary of Slang and Unconventional English,* 8th ed., ed. Paul Beale (New York: Macmillan, 1984), s.vv. "what cheer."

15. On *wha cheer netop,* see James Axtell, "Babel of Tongues: Communicating with the Indians in Eastern North America," in *The Language Encounter in the Americas, 1492–1800: A Collection of Essays*, ed. Edward G. Gray and Norman Fiering (New York: Berghahn Books, 2000), 34. The phrase *what cheer netop* is a greeting probably derived from the Narragansett pidginization of the English phrase "What cheer?" and the Narragansett word for brother or friend. *Netop* became a word in American-English much as *neechee* (originally from the Ojibwa language) in Canadian-English.

16. Roger H. Durand, *Some Interesting Notes about Indians* (Rehoboth, Mass.: Durand and Co., 1991), 124. Other relevant books from Durand include *Notes about Christmas* (1993) and *Interesting Notes about Allegorical Representations* (1994).

17. Job Durfee, *What Cheer; or, Roger Williams in Banishment: A poem,* rev. and ed. Thomas Durfee (Providence: Preston and Rounds, 1896), 54.

18. On the "imaging of Indians," see, for example, Elise Marienstras, "The Common Man's Indian: The Image of the Indian as a Promoter of National Identity in the Early National Era"; Vivien Green Fryd, "Imaging the Indians in the United States Capitol during the Early Republic"; and James H. Merrell, "American Nations, Old and New: Reflections on Indians and the Early Republic." All three essays appear in *Native Americans and the Early Republic,* ed. Frederick E. Hoxie, Ronald Hoffman, and Peter J. Albert (Charlottesville: University Press of Virginia, 1999).

Chapter 4: Coins on Paper

The epigraph is from Poe's story "The Gold-Bug," first published in the *Dollar Newspaper* (June 21, June 28, and July 12, 1843). Here quoted from Thomas Ollive Mabbott, ed., *The Collected Works of Edgar Allan Poe* (Cambridge, Mass.: Belknap Press of Harvard University Press, 1978).

1. Among the many relatively recent books on this subject, see Jennifer J. Baker, *Securing the Commonwealth: Debt, Speculation, and Writing in the Marking of Early America* (Baltimore: Johns Hopkins University Press, 2005). Baker does not mention wampum.

2. On Poe's short story, see Shell, "The Gold Bug."

3. Carlos Ortuño, *Historia Numismática del Ecuador* (Quito: Banco Central del Ecuador, 1978), says that a total of 402,649 eight-escudos coins were produced between 1838 and 1840. On the semiotic role of the doubloon in Melville, see Shell, *Economy of Literature,* 83–85.

4. The catostomus fish *Sclerognathus* [or *Cycleptus*] *elongatus* is a sucker found in the Mississippi and Ohio Rivers. See also George Brown Goode, *American Fishes: A Popular Treatise Upon the Game and Food Dishes of North America* (New York: Houghton, 1888), 436: "The Black Horse, . . . also called 'Missouri Sucker', . . . 'Suckerel' and 'Shoenaher.'"

5. See A. H. Saxon, *P. T. Barnum: The Legend and the Man* (New York: Columbia University Press, 1989), 335–36.

6. This text was used at the Boston Latin School during the time that Harris Gray Otis, later senator from Massachusetts, studied there with John Lovell, who was the school's master. "Colonial Schooling and School Administration" (1907), at http://www.oldandsold.com/articles24/school-management-26.shtml, accessed February 18, 2008.

7. Williams, *Key into the Language of America,* 147.

8. Williams writes, "Their owne [money] is of two sorts: one white, which they make of the stem or stocke of the Periwinkle, . . . and of this sort six of their small Beads . . . are currant with the English for a peny. The second is black, inclining to blew, which is made of the shell of a fish, which some English call Hens, Poquauhock, and of this sort three make an English peny." Ibid., 144.

Chapter 5: What Is Wampum?

The epigraphs are from William Wood, "A Small Nomenclator of the Indian Language," *New England's Prospect* (1634; repr., Amherst: University of Massachusetts Press, 1977), 118; and Francis Parkman, *France and England in North America: A Series of Historical Narratives,* part 2, *The Jesuits in North America in the Seventeenth Century* (Boston: Little, Brown, 1867), xxxi.

1. Samuel Peckworth Woodward, *A Manual of the Mollusca* (London: J. Weale, 1856), 305.

2. See Robert E. Stearns, *Ethno-Conchology: A Study of Primitive Money,* Smithsonian Institution Report, part 2 (1887) (Washington, D.C.: Government Printing Office, 1889), 297–334.

3. Gunther Michelson, "Iroquoian Terms for Wampum," *International Journal of American Linguistics* 57.1 (January 1991): 108–16.

4. See Sébastien Rasles, *A Dictionary of the Abnaki Language in North America,* published from the original manuscript, introd. John Pickering (Cambridge, Mass.: C. Folsom, 1833). The manuscript is preserved at Harvard University.

5. Some Mohawks call the cylindrical beads *onehkohra,* as Jean-André Cuoq, in his *Lexique de la langue algonquine* (Montréal: J. Chapleau, 1886), 68, points out, with a discussion also of the Algonquian *mikis.* For further discussion of the Iroquoian terms for wampum, see Michelson, "Iroquoian Terms for Wampum," 108–31. The Algonquian word *roanoke* is sometimes translated to mean "to rub," "abrade," "smooth" or "polish" (as in making roanoke, peak or wampum beads). See *The Roanoke Voyages, 1584–1590: Documents to Illustrate the English Voyages to North America Under the Patent Granted to Walter Raleigh in 1584,* ed. David Beers Quinn (New York: Dover, 1991), 104–5.

6. Certain French writers—among them Joseph Pierre Anselme Maurault in his *Histoire des Abénakis, depuis 1605 jusqu'à nos jours* (Sorel, Québec: Imprimé à l'atelier typographique de la "Gazette de Sorel," 1866)—consider the actual Abnaki term, which Marrault himself transcribes as *8ânbôbi.* Maurault uses the symbol *8* to indicate the sound "ou" (or "w" before a vowel), *ân* to indicate "aiénné," and the character *ô* to indicate the sound "on"—as he explains in the two (unnumbered) pages of the preface to his book, "Quelques règles pour aider à prononcer les mots Abénakis." On *mikis,* see Jean-André Cuoq, *Lexique de la langue algonquine* (Montréal: J. Chapleau, 1886), 68. Edward Francis Wilson, in his *Ojebway Language: A Manuel for Missionaries and Others Employed among the Ojebway Indians* (Toronto: Printed by Rowsell and Hutchinson for the Venerable Society for Promoting Christian Knowledge, London, 1874), 265, points to *megis* and variants.

7. Lorraine E. Williams and Karen A. Flinn, *Trade Wampum: New Jersey to the Plains* (Trenton, N.J.: New Jersey State Museum, 1990).

8. "Wampum collars" in certain Iroquoian dialects were called *gaionne,* according to the writers in 1847 of the Civil Code of Canada. See especially chapter 2, "An Act to permit the importation of Wampum from the Neighbouring States by the Inland communication of Lake Champlain and the River Richelieu or Sorel," in *Laws of Lower-Canada, under the constitution, erected 26th December, Anno Domini, 1791, pursuant to act of Parliament [Loix du Bas-Canada, sous la constitution érigée le 26 décembre Anno Domini 1791, en consequence d'un acte du Parlement] Lower Canada. Laws, etc.* (Québec: Published by order of the government, by William Vondenvelden, 1794), 3.

9. Jacques Cartier, *Voyage de J. Cartier au Canada* [Paris: Librairie Tross, 1863], section titled "Comment le cappitaine & les gentilz hommes avec vingt cinq hommes bien armez & en bon ordre, allerent en la ville de Hochelaga & la situacion dudict lieu," 24. The translation comes from Robert Kerr and F. A. S. Eden, *A General History and Collection of Voyages and Travels,* 18 vols. (Edinburgh: W. Blackwood, 1811–24), vol. 6, section titled "The Second Voyage of Jacques Cartier, to Canada, Hochelega, Saguenay, and Other Lands Now Called New France; with the Manners and Customs of the Natives." The item described there is probably not wampum per se. For an English-language translation, see Cartier, *A Vocabulary of Stadaconan: From the First and Second Relations of Jacques Cartier. Including a Word-List from Hochelaga* (Southampton, Pa.: Evolution Pub., 1999); this is a reprint from H. P. Biggar's translation *The Voyages of Jacques Cartier* (Ottawa: F. A. Acland, printer, 1924). William Dawson, in his *Nouvelle note sur les antiquités aborigines trouvés* (Montréal, 1850s), 31, notes that what we called *wampum* is what Jacques Cartier reports as *esurgny,* a term that the French-Canadian short-story writer and lexicographer Sylva Clapin takes up in *Dictionnaire canadien-français ou Lexique-glossaire des mots, expressions et locutions ne se trouvant pas dans les dictionnaires courants et dont l'usage appartient surtout aux Canadiens-français* (Montréal: C. Beauchemain, 1894), 336.

10. Hale, "Four Huron Wampum Records," 224.

11. The translators often disagree with one another about whether the appropriate translation for Champlain's "French" term *pourcelaine* should be the "English" term *porcelain* (which is what Charles Pomeroy Otis prefers in his translation, *Voyages of Samuel Champlain,* illus. Edmund F. Slafter [Boston: Prince Society, 1878–82]) or the "English" term *wampum* (which is what one finds in Annie Nettleton Bourne's translation, *Voyages and Explorations of Samuel de Champain,* introd. Edward Gaylord Bourne [New York: A. S. Barnes, 1922]).

12. Maurault, *Histoire des Abenakis,* came to prefer what was called the "English" term *wampum* because *porcelain* was associated with the earthenware and counterfeitness that the French traders introduced into the wampum systems (27).

13. Herbert Stanley Jevons, *Money and the Mechanism of Exchange* (London: H. S. King, 1875), 24.

14. Randall Herbert Balmer, *A Perfect Babel of Confusion: Dutch Religion and English Culture in the Middle Colonies* (New York: Oxford University Press, 1989).

15. Adriaen Cornelissen van der Donck, "Van der Donck's Description of New-Netherlands," *Collections of the New-York Historical Society,* 2d ser., vol. 1 (New York: the Society, 1841), 206. For the original, see Van der Donck, *Beschryvinge van Nieuw-Nederlant* (Amsterdam: Evert Nieuwenhof, 1656).

16. Mary W. Harman, "Wampum as Money in Northeastern North America," *Ethnohistory* 3.1 (1956): 21–33, points out that wampum did *not* become legal tender in New France. See the discussion of playing-card money in New France in Shell, *Art and Money* (Chicago: University of Chicago Press, 1995), 82–83, 87.

17. Edmund Bailey O'Callaghan, ed., *Documents Relative to the Colonial History of the State of New York,* 15 vols. (Albany: Weed, Parsons, 1853–57), 10:556.

18. On Marx's theory of the *Warensprache* (language of commodities), see Marx, *Das Kapital,* in Karl Marx and Friedrich Engels, *Werke,* ed. Institut für Marxismus-Leninismus beim ZK der SED (Berlin: Dietz, 1956–68), 23:66–67, 97 (translated as *Capital,* trans. S. Moore and E. Aveling [New York: International Publishers, 1967], 1:52, 83), and Marx, "Auszüge aus James Mills Buch 'Elémens d'economie politique,'" in Marx and Engels, *Werke,* Ergänzungsband, pt. 1, 461. See also Shell, *Money, Language, and Thought,* ch. 4.

19. Parker, *Mrs. Falchion,* 118. For a relevant (and contemporary) treatment of Chinook Jargon, see Shaw, *Chinook Jargon and How to Use It.* For the counterpart Choctaw trading language, see my forthcoming *Painting in the Trash Bin.*

20. Marc Lescarbot's map of New France (1618) includes the fleurs de lys at Port Royal; see his *Histoire de la Nouvelle-France* (Paris: Chez Adrian Peter, 1618); see "Figvure de la Terre Nevve . . ." On the crests, see *Loyalist Souvenir: One Hundred and Fiftieth Anniversary of the Landing of the Loyalists in the Province of New Brunswick 1783–1933* (Saint John, N.B., Can.: New Brunswick Historical Society, [1933]), esp. the article on settlement by William F. Ganong.

21. John Richardson, *Tecumseh, or, The Warrior of the West* (London: Printed for R. Glynn, 1828; repr., Ottawa, Canada: Golden Dog, 1978), 44.

22. J. Hammond Trumbull, *On Some Words Derived from Languages of the North American Indians* (American Philological Association, 1872), 5.

23. Claude-Charles Le Roy Bacqueville de la Potherie, *Histoire de l'Amérique septentrionale* (Paris: Jean-Luc Nion et François Didot, 1722), 34. The translation from the French is by Nancy Shawcross.

24. For the Penn Belt, see Frank G. Speck, *The Penn Wampum Belts* (New York: De Vinne, 1925), example 4. On the Washington Covenant Belt, see Noah T. Clarke, *The Wampum Belt Collection of the New York State Museum,* New York State Museum Bulletin 228 (Albany: University of the State of New York, 1931): 85–121. Clarke reports that the Washington Covenant Belt was used during the presidency of George Washington as a covenant of peace between the Thirteen Original Colonies and the Six Nations of the Iroquois. For the Oneida Tribal Belt, see E. W. Paige, "Readings of the Wampums of the Five Nations by Te-hes-ha (Daniel La Fort) and the Reverend Thomas La Fort, at Onondaga Castle. 19 July, 1898, and 1 August, 1898," Appellate div. sup. Court 4th dep't. Onondaga nation *et al.,* vs. J. B. Thacher; Papers on appeal, p. 56.

Chapter 6: Indian Giving and Willie Wampum

The epigraph is from James Fenimore Cooper, *The Last of the Mohicans: A Narrative of 1757* (Philadelphia: Carey and Lea, 1826), ch. 30.

1. Harriet Maxwell Converse's remark was quoted in William Martin Beauchamp, *Wampum and Shell Articles Used by the New York Indians* (Albany: University of the State of New York, 1901), 428. See also the discussion of uses in Elizabeth S. Peña, "Wampum Production." On the role of wampum in gift giving, see Cornelius J. Janen, "The Role of Presents in French-Amerindian Trade," in *Explorations in Canadian Economic History: Essays in Honour of Irene M. Spry,* ed. Duncan Cameron (Ottawa: University of Ottawa Press, 1985), 231–50.

2. As an example, consider Backhaus: "The functions of wampum were far more complex than the numismatic and aesthetic functions of the European precious metals." Gary Backhaus, "Indian Gaming," ms., 12–13, Collection Selechonek.

3. For this latter view, see Lewis Hyde, *The Gift: Imagination and the Erotic Life of Property* (New York: Vintage, 1983).

4. Wood, "A Small Nomenclator," 118.

5. Mark Twain, *Life on the Mississippi* (Boston: J. R. Osgood, 1883; repr., New York: Harper and Bros., 1901), Appendix D: "The Undying Head," 456.

6. *OED*, s.v. "giver" A4, has only the second meaning, and American dictionaries, including John Russell Bartlett, *Dictionary of Americanisms: A Glossary of Words and Phrases Usually Regarded as Peculiar to the United States* (Boston: Little, Brown, 1859), also have this meaning. The American dictionaries usually also have the first meaning.

7. Thomas Hutchinson, *The History of the Colony of Massachusets-Bay, from the first settlement thereof in 1628, until its incorporation with the colony of Plimouth, Province of Main, &c. by the charter of King William and Queen Mary, in 1691, 2nd ed.* (London: Printed for Richardson, 1765): 1.469n.

8. See my discussion in chapter 8 of the present book.

9. See Shell, *Art and Money*.

10. For an elaboration of this argument, see ibid., ch. 2.

11. For the theology at work here and its relationship to the idea of grace in popular culture, see Shell, "The Blank Check," in *Money, Language, and Thought*, 24–46.

12. Tzvetan Todorov, *The Conquest of America: The Question of the Other* (New York: Harper and Row, 1984), 221.

13. Ala Alryyes, "'And in a Christian Language They Sold Me': Messages Concealed in a Slave's Arabic-Language Autobiographical Narrative," in *American Babel: Literatures of the United States from Abnaki to Zuni*, ed. Marc Shell (Cambridge, Mass.: Harvard University Press, 2002), 41–54; and "The Life of Omar Ibn Said, Written by Himself," trans. and introd. Ala Alryyes, in *The Multilingual Anthology of American Literature*, ed. Marc Shell and Werner Sollors (New York: NYU Press, 2000), 58–93.

14. See Shell, *Art and Money*, 57. See also Charles de Brosses, *Le Culte des Dieux fétiches; ou, Parallèle de l'ancienne religion de l'Egypte avec la religion actuelle de Nigrite* ([Paris?]: n.p., 1760). Writes Edward Meirion Roberts in *Flying Fighter: An American above the Lines in France* (New York: Harper, 1918), 328: "Each man had his own little fetish. It was known as the pocket-piece or mascot. In some cases it might be a dice or a playing-card. . . . In other cases it might be a locket, then again a medal."

15. *OED*, s.v. "mascot."

16. *OED*, s.v. "totem," 1-a. For more on the tradition named, see Claude Lévi-Strauss, *Le Totémisme aujourd'hui* (Paris: Presses Universitaires de France, 1962).

17. See M. Landreth, "Becoming the Indians: Fashioning Arkansas State University's Indians," in *Team Spirits: Essays on the History and Significance of Native American Mascots*, ed. C. Richard King and Charles Fruehling Springwood, foreword by Vine Deloria (Lincoln: University of Nebraska Press, 2001), 46–63.

18. See C. Richard King, "Uneasy Indians: Creating and Contesting Native American Mascots at Marquette University," in King and Springwood, *Team Spirits*, 281–303.

19. Joseph Wright, *The English Dialect Dictionary* (London: H. Frowde, 1905), suppl., 178, col. 2, s.v. "Willy."

20. See Gregor Ian Smith, *The Story of Willie Wampum: A Red Indian Boy* (London and Glasgow: Blackie and Son, 1955).

21. Howard Hawks, dir., *Monkey Business* (1952), to be distinguished from the Marx Brothers' *Monkey Business* (1931).

22. William Makepeace Thackeray, *The Virginians: A Tale of the Last Century* (New York: Harper, 1859), ch. 51, "Conticuere Omnes," 223; Oliphant, *Episodes in a Life of Adventure; or, Moss from a Rolling Stone* (New York: Harper and Brothers, 1887), 70. On American Indians represented as speaking with *ughs,* see also Warren F. Broderick, "New York State's Mohicans in Literature," *Hudson River Valley Review: A Journal of Regional Studies* 19.2 (September 2002): 7.

23. See, for example, Cooper, *Last of the Mohicans,* ch. 26.

24. See, for example, *The Jack Benny Show* for December 9, 1951 (CD obtained from Old Time Radio Now [www.otrnow.com]).

25. Wendell Johnson, "The Indians Have No Word for It: Stuttering in Children," *Quarterly Journal of Speech* 30 (1944): 330–37. The opposite (and relatively accurate) position is presented by Joseph Letie Stewart, *The Problem of Stuttering in Certain North American Indian Societies, Journal of Speech and Hearing Disorders* monograph supplement 6 (Washington, D.C.: American Speech and Hearing Association, 1960).

26. *Sunday at Home* 504 (May 1923) 3. This publication was a "family magazine for Sabbath reading" published by the Religious Tract Society.

Chapter 7: Money Writing

The epigraph is from John Gottlieb Ernestus Heckewelder, *An Account of the History, Manners, and Customs of the Indian Nations, Who Once Inhabited Pennsylvania and the Neighbouring States* (Philadelphia: Abraham Small, 1819; rev ed., Philadelphia: Historical Society of Pennsylvania, 1876), 108 (all quotations are from the 1876 ed.).

1. The term *India* or *New India* often referred to "North America," following here the Portuguese and Spanish tradition. See Richard Eden, *A Treatise of the New India* (London: E. Sutton, 1553), and Samuel Purchas, *Pilgrimage* (London: Printed by William Stansby for Henrie Fetherstone, 1613), esp. 451: "The name of India, is now applied to all farre-distant Countries, not in the extreme limits of Asia alone; but even to whole America, through the errour of Columbus . . . who . . . in the Westerne world, thought that they had met with Ophir, and the Indian Regions of the East." The term *West Indies* still exists.

2. See Georges E. Sioui, *Pour une autohistoire amérindienne. Essai sur les fondements d'une morale sociale* (Québec: Les Presses de l'Université Laval, 1989).

3. On living symbols, see Paul Williams, "Reading Wampum Belts as Living Symbols" *Northeast Indian Quarterly* 7.1 (Spring 1990): 31–35. On nonanimate, or inanimate, nouns, see David A. Francis Sr. and Robert M. Leavitt, eds., *A Maliseet-Passamaquoddy Dictionary,* s.v. "Wapap," http://www.lib.unb.ca/Texts/Maliseet/dictionary, accessed August 12, 2005. Note, however, that *wapi-man* ("[metal] silver; silver money [collectively])" is an inanimate noun, and *wapi-maniyey* ("something silver; [animate] silver coin") can be both animate and inanimate.

4. Martien, *Shell Game,* for example, emphasizes that *wampum* is an animate noun in many Algonquian languages (10), but he neglects to do a thorough philological or comparative study.

5. Conor McDonough Quinn, "A Preliminary Survey of Animacy Categories in Penobscot," in *Papers of the 32nd Algonquian Conference,* ed. John D. Nichols (Winnipeg: University of Manitoba, 2001),

395–426; a version of this is available at http://conormquin.com/Animacy2004.pdf (accessed January 6, 2013), where the quoted material falls on 23n67.

6. Ibid., 23n66 (Web site).

7. Henry David Thoreau, "The Allegash and East Branch," *The Maine Woods* (Boston: Ticknor and Fields, 1864), 161.

8. On marriage belts in general, see Frank G. Speck, *The Functions of Wampum among the Eastern Algonkian* (Lancaster, Pa.: American Anthropological Association, 1919).

9. See Quinn, "Preliminary Survey," 23n66 (Web site). For Eckstorm's comment, see Fannie Hardy Eckstorm, *Old John Neptune and Other Maine Indian Shamans* (Portland, Me.: Southworth-Anthoensen, 1945), 193.

10. See, for example, Speck, *The Functions of Wampum.*

11. See Joseph Laurent, *New Familiar Abenakis and English Dialogues: The First Ever Published on the Grammatical System* (Québec: L. Brousseau, 1884).

12. For a discussion and examples of "pendants" and "runtees," see Robert Beverley, *History of Virginia* (London: B. and S. Tooke, 1722), 145.

13. *Wapapi Akonutomakonol: The Wampum Records: Wabanaki Traditional Laws,* as recounted by Lewis Mitchell (1897), revised, annotated, and edited and with a new translation by Robert M. Leavit and David A. Francis (Fredericton, N.B., Can.: Micmac-Maliseet Institute, University of New Brunswick, 1990). Here the wampum are records printed in both English and Passamaquoddy languages. When it comes to studying the Lakota, the situation is the same. Few students of the "Plains Indians" bother to consult the Lakota writings. Among writings to consult relevant to our period is the newspaper *Anpao* (The Day Breaks), which was published from 1878 to 1886 by the Niobrara Mission in Yankton, South Dakota. See too recent works by Ella Cara Deloria.

14. Alice Morse Earle, in *The Sabbath in Puritan New England* (1891), reports in chapter 10, "The Deacon's Office," that Thomas Lechford, in his *Plain dealing, or, News from New-England: A short view of New-Englands present government, both ecclesiasticall and civil, compared with the anciently-received and established government of England in some materiall points. Fit for the gravest consideration in these times* (London: Printed by W. E. and I. G. for N. Butter, 1642), is worried about the dishonesty of his coreligionists in Boston and "publicly warned, as the records show, that they must deposit "wampum without break or deforming spots," or "passable peage without breaches." Earle, *The Sabbath in Puritan New England,* 7th ed. (Whitefish, Mont.: Kessinger, 2004), 65.

15. George Bancroft, *History of the United States of America from the Discovery of the Continent [to 1789],* 6 vols. (Boston: Little, 1876), 2:183.

16. In 1693, "the ferriage for each single person from New York to Brooklyn was eight styvers in wampum, or a silver two-pence." Edmund Bailey O'Callaghan, *History of New Netherland, or New York, under the Dutch* (New York: D. Appleton, 1846–48), 1:61, quoted in Beauchamp, *Wampum and Shell Articles,* 356.

17. Isaías Lerner, "Spanish Colonization and the Indigenous Languages of America," in *Language Encounter,* ed. Gray and Fiering, esp. 282–86.

18. Axtell, "Babel of Tongues," 48.

19. Johannes Fabian, *Language and Colonial Power: The Appropriation of Swahili in the Former Belgian Congo 1880–1938* (Cambridge: Cambridge University Press, 1986), 51.

20. Axtell, "Babel of Tongues," 46.

21. On John Montour, see Randolph C. Downes, *Council Fires on the Upper Ohio: A Narrative of Indian Affairs in the Upper Ohio Valley until 1795* (Pittsburgh: University of Pittsburgh Press, 1940), 192–93.

22. Axtell, "Babel of Tongues," 51. See also Ives Goddard, "The Use of Pidgins and Jargons on the East Coast of North America," in *Language Encounter,* ed. Gray and Fiering, 70.

23. Axtell, "Babel of Tongues," 40.

24. Eskimo trade jargon was used in the nineteenth century by Inuit when dealing with whites and members of other Native American groups on Copper Island in the Aleutian Islands. Mednyj Aleut was used in the nineteenth century by descendants of a mixed Russian-Aleut population in the Aleutian Islands. Chinook Jargon was used during the first half of the nineteenth century by Native Americans and white settlers in the Northwest along the Pacific Coast. Michif (Metchif, Métis, and French Cree) is used currently by descendants of French-speaking fur traders and Algonquian women on the Turtle Mountain Reservation in North Dakota. In South America, Nheengatu (or Lingua Geral Amazonica) developed in northern Brazil for communication among people of Native American, European, and African origin. For the Choctaw Mobilian trade language, see ch. 10, n. 36.

25. Rüdiger Schreyer, "'Savage' Languages in Eighteenth-Century Theoretical History of Language," in *Language Encounter,* ed. Gray and Fiering, 320.

26. Quoted in Tehanetorens (Ray Fadden), *Wampum Belts of the Iroquois* (Summertown, Tenn.: Book Pub., 1999), 74.

27. Hale, "Four Huron Wampum Records," 227.

28. Fabian, *Language and Colonial Power,* 51.

29. For the Ojibwa grave posts, see John McLean, "Picture-Writing of the Blackfeet" (1894), *Transactions of the Canadian Institute,* vol. 5 (Toronto: printed for the Institute by Murray Printing Co., 1898), 114–20. The origin of the Mi'kmaq hieroglyphs—whether partly indigenous or wholly Jesuit inspired—is not yet completely understood. See Bruce Greenfield, "The Mi'kmaq Hieroglyphic Prayer Book: Writing and Christianity in Maritime Canada, 1675–1921," in *Language Encounter*, ed. Gray and Fiering, 189–211. On wampum, see Barbara A. Mann, "The Fire at Onondaga: Wampum as Proto-Writing," *Akwesasne Notes* 1.1 (Spring 1995): 40–48.

30. On the Indian writing issue, see Germaine Warkentin, "In Search of 'The Word of the Other': Aboriginal Sign Systems and the History of the Book in Canada," *Book History* 2.1 (1999): 1–27. See also Garrick Mallery, *Picture-Writing of the American Indians* (1893; repr., New York: Dover, 1972); and Dana Leibsohn, "Mapping after the Letter: Graphology and Indigenous Cartography in New Spain," in *Language Encounter,* ed. Gray and Fiering, 128.

31. William Johnson, "Sir Wm Johnson to the Rev'd Dr. Auchmuty" (May 27, 1770), in *The Documentary History of the State of New-York,* dir. Christopher Morgan, ed. E. B. O'Callaghan, 4 vols. (Albany: Charles Benthuysen, 1849–51), 4:434: "This chief of a whole nation has the custody of the belts of wampum, &c. which are as records of public transactions." See also *The Papers of Sir William Johnson* (Albany: State University of New York, 1962). For a fascinating overview of wampum belts in this context, see also Tehanetorens, *Wampum Belts.*

32. Thomas Carlyle, *Critical and Miscellaneous Essays* (Boston: Phillips, Sampson, 1857), vol. 2, 168 (attrib.).

33. See John Wolfe Lydekker, *Faithful Mohawks* (Cambridge: Cambridge University Press, 1938),

27: "And as a sure Token of the sincerity of the six Nations, We do . . . present Our Great Queen with these Belts of Wampum" (1710).

34. Mary A. Druke, introd., *Iroquois Indians Microforms: A Documentary History of the Diplomacy of the Six Nations and Their League,* ed. Francis Jennings and William N. Fenton, D'Arcy McNickle Center for the History of the American Indian, Newberry Library (Woodbridge, Conn.: Research Publications, 1985); v–xi. See also Peña, "Wampum Production," 34.

35. Walter Hoffman, *Beginnings of Writing,* introd. Fred Starr (New York: Appleton, 1895): 24. Parkman, who usually relies on works (mostly Algonquian) edited by Henry Rowe Schoolcraft, writes, "The belts, on occasions of importance, were wrought into significant devices, suggestive of the substance of the compact or speech, and designed as aids to memory. . . . The figures on wampum-belts were, for the most part, simply mnemonic. So also were those carved on wooden tablets, or painted on bark and skin, to preserve in memory the songs of war, hunting, or magic." However, in certain cases, he sees more: "The Hurons had, however, in common with other tribes, a system of rude pictures and arbitrary signs, by which they could convey to each other, with tolerable precision, information touching the ordinary subjects of Indian interest." Parkman, *France and England in North America,* part 2, *Jesuits in North America,* xxxii.

36. John Lubbock, *Prehistoric Times as Illustrated by Ancient Remains and the Manners and Customs of Modern Savages* (London: Williams and Norgate, 1865), writes, "The art of picture-writing . . . was supplemented among the North American Indians by the 'wampum'" (227).

37. See Jonathan C. Lainey, *La "Monnaie des Sauvages": Les colliers de wampum d'hier à aujourd'hui* (Sillery, Québec: Septentrion, 2004), example 43.

38. In addition to Zacharie de Pazzide Bonneville, *De l'Amérique et des Américains, ou observations curieuses du philosophe La Douceur, Qui a parcouru ce Hémisphere pendant la dernière Guerre, en faisant le noble métier de tuer des Hommes sans les manger* (Berlin: Samuel Pitram, 1772), 86–87, see Aren Akweks, *Key to Indian Pictographs* (Hogansburg, N.Y.: St. Regis Mohawk Reservation, Akwesasne Counselor Organization, [194?]); Arthur Einhorn, "Iroquois-Algonquin Wampum Exchanges and Preservation in the 20th Century: A Case for in-situ Preservation," *Man in the Northeast* 7 (Spring 1974), esp. 81; and Lainey, *La "Monnaie des Sauvages,"* 168–71.

39. Merrell, *Into the American Woods,* 193.

40. Sir William Johnson to Arthur Lee, 1771, in *Documentary History of the State of New York,* ed. O'Callaghan, 4:269–74, quoted in Beauchamp, *Wampum and Shell Articles,* 395.

41. Vincent Wilcox, "The Manufacture and Use of Wampum in the Northeast," unpublished paper, 1972, quoted in Martien, *Shell Game,* 22n ("symbol of the power of the word"); Arthur Caswell Parker, in *Constitution of the Five Nations; or, The Iroquois Book of the Great Law,* New York State Museum Bulletin no. 184, (Albany: University of the State of New York, 1916), 6, reports the saying of Hiawatha (or Hayonhwatha) quoted in Martien, *Shell Game,* 70. For a discussion of various legends involving Hiawatha and wampum, see Beauchamp, *Wampum and Shell Articles,* 339–41.

42. The *Cherokee Phoenix,* the first newspaper published by American Indians, greeted its first readers in both Cherokee and English in 1828. The Cherokee press also published biblical passages, hymnals, and other tracts.

43. In the *Annual Report of the Director of the Mint to the Secretary of the Treasury for the Fiscal Year ended June 30, 1863* (Philadelphia: Bryson and Son, 1864), it was said, "But it may here be stated, that several

specimens of Mormon coinage of gold five-dollar pieces, dated 1860, have lately appeared here. They are entirely different in devices from the coinage executed at Salt Lake City in 1849. On one side the legend is 'Deseret Assay Office,' and on the other sundry cabalistic characters. They have undergone no improvement as to intrinsic value."

44. For the quoted phrase, see George William Grace, *Linguistic Construction of Reality* (London: Croom Helm, 1897).

45. See the general discussion in Julia M. Penn, *Linguistic Relativity versus Innate Ideas: Origins of the Sapir-Whorf Hypothesis in German Thought* (The Hague: Mouton, 1972). See also Benjamin Whorf, *The Hopi Language* (Chicago: University of Chicago Library, 1965 [microform]); and Edward Sapir, *American Indian Languages* (Berlin: Mouton de Gruyter, 1990–91).

46. For this formulation of one side of the issue, see Cynthia Hsin-feng Wu, "Can You Think About What You Don't Talk About?" Qualifying Paper, RLLD, Harvard Graduate School of Education, 1991.

47. The word *wampum* was absorbed not only by the English. The term was "adopted (in 16–17th c.) from the northerly dials. of the Algonquin language" (*OED*, s.v. "wampum"). Such reference works as Sébastien Rasles's *Abnaki Dictionary* (1691) list variations of the pronunciation and spelling involving both Indian and European dialectical differences. The *OED* cites Rasles as defining *wambambi* (pl. -ak) as "grain blan de porcelaine" and *wambambiar* as "chapelet"; following Zeisberger, it defines the Delaware word *wapapi* as "white wampum" and *woapaschapiall* as "white beads." The word for black beads was never brought over into English.

48. Benjamin Franklin Decosta, *Hiawatha; or, The Story of the Iroquois Sage in Prose and Verse* (New York: A. D. F. Randolph and Co., 1873).

49. On the success of Longfellow's publication, see ibid. For a fine analysis of the reception of this poem, see Alan Trachtenberg, *Shades of Hiawatha: Staging Indians, Making Americans, 1880–1930* (New York: Hill and Wang, 2004), esp. ch. 1. The relevant role of wampum in literature and folklore is touched on by George S. Snyderman, "An Ethnological Discussion of Allegany Seneca Wampum Folklore," *Proceedings of the American Philosophical Society* 126.4 (August 1982): 316–26. For the Ojibwa translation, see L. O. Armstrong, *Hiawatha or Nanahbozo* (Montréal, 1901).

50. Longfellow presided over Harvard's modern-language program for eighteen years; he left teaching in 1854.

51. Consider here the artwork of painters such as Karen Yxomme Lynch Harley, for example, her *Keeper of Wampum,* a painting that incorporates trompe l'oeil; author's correspondence with Harley, March 12, 2005.

52. See Hazel W. Hertzberg, *The Search for an American Indian Identity: Modern Pan-Indian Movements* (Syracuse, N.Y.: Syracuse University Press, 1971), 215–16, 336. See also Pat Montague's not untypical novel *The Wampum Keeper* (Markham, Ont., Can.: Double Dragon Publishing, 2000).

53. See James B. LaGrand, *Indian Metropolis: Native Americans in Chicago, 1945–75* (Urbana: University of Illinois Press, 2002). The Grand Council Fire—later renamed the Indian Council Fire—operated in the Chicago area from the 1920s to the 1950s; it eventually became so nostalgically romantic as to call its treasurer "Chief Wampum Keeper." Elsewhere too the term *wampum keeper* became an almost permanently misplaced cultural signpost; see David R. M. Beck, "The Chicago American Indian Community," in *Native Chicago,* ed. Terry Straus and Grant P. Arndt (Chicago: Native Chicago, 1998), 167–81.

Chapter 8: Civilization

The epigraph is from *The Writings of Thomas Jefferson,* ed. Bergh, 15:185.

1. John Smith, *The Generall Historie of Virginia, New England and the Summer Isles,* vol. 1 (1624; Glasgow: John MacLehose and Sons, 1907), 121.

2. Louis Martin Sears, "The Puritan and His Indian Ward," *American Journal of Sociology* 22 (July 1916): 80.

3. John Adams to F. A. Vanderkemp, February 16, 1809, in *Works of John Adams,* 10 vols., ed. Charles Francis Adams (Boston: Little, Brown, 1856), 9:610.

4. Jefferson, in *Writings of Thomas Jefferson,* ed. Bergh, 15:185.

5. Useful material is represented in Gray and Fiering's *Language Encounter,* but my material is adapted to the problem of monetary (as well as linguistic) translation.

6. Merrell, *Into the American Woods,* writes, "They were the ones who carried the letters, but did not sign and seal them; who memorized the speech on wampum belts, but did not draft it; who translated, but did not speak, at the grand councils; who stood between the tables crowded with colonial and Indian leaders at a treaty banquet to make sure that the liquor and talk flowed freely, but did not join the feast" (33). Compare the experience of the *métis* John Montour, as reported in Downes, *Council Fires.* On the general notion here of go-between, see also Nancy L. Hagedorn, "Brokers of Understanding: Interpreters as Agents of Cultural Exchange in Colonial New York," *New York History* 76.4 (1995): 399–400.

7. One account of this meeting goes as follows: "M. [Jacques] de Meulles, the [French Intendant], gave a somewhat critical account of the meeting at La Famine [at the mouth of the Salmon River] in a letter to M. Seignelay, dated Quebec 10 Oct. 1684, 'There came altogether on this embassy only a certain sycophant who seeks merely a good dinner, and a real buffoon, called among the French la Grande Gueule, accompanied by eight or ten miserable fellows, who fooled the General in a most shameful manner, as you will perceive by the articles of peace I have the honor to send you, and which I doubt not he also will send you.'" Tomas Grassmann, "OTREAOUTI," in *Dictionary of Canadian Biography Online,* http://www.biographi.ca/009004–119.01-e.php?&id_nbr=495, accessed January 6, 2013.

8. Big Mouth, also known as Otreouti Hateouati, Hoteouate, Hotrehouati, Houtreouati, Oureouhat, and Outreouhati, was called "La Grande Gueule" ("Big Mouth"), hence also "Grangular" or "Grangula."

9. See Louis Armand Lahontan, *Nouveaux Voyages dans l'Amérique septentrionale,* 2 vols. (The Hague: Les frères L'Honoré, 1703), trans. as *New Voyages to North America* (London: H. Bonwicke, T. Goodwin, M. Wotton, B. Tooke, and S. Manship, 1705).

10. See Dale Miquelon, *New France: A Supplement to Europe (1701–1744),* Canadian Centennial Series 4 (Toronto: McLelland and Stewart, 1987). See also Ernest Zay, *Numismatique coloniale—Canada: La Monnaie de carte* (Paris: Société française de numismatique, 1889).

11. Newman, *The Early Paper Money of America* (Racine, Wisc.: Whitman, 1967), 7.

12. Joseph-François Lafitau, *Customs of the American Indians Compared with the Customs of Primitive Times,* trans. William N. Fenton and Elizabeth L. Moore, 2 vols. (Toronto: Champlain Society, 1974–77), 1:310–11. Lafitau's book was first published as *Moeurs des sauvages amériquains comparées aux moeurs des premiers temps* (Paris: Saugrain l'aîné, C. E. Hochereau, 1724).

13. Heckewelder, *An Account of the History, Manners, and Customs of the Indian Nations,* 108. Quoted in

William Fenton, *The Great Law and the Longhouse: A Political History of the Iroquois Confederacy* (Norman: University of Oklahoma Press, 1998), 233.

14. See Henri Beau's drawing *Playing Card Money,* National Archives of Canada, C-17059.

15. Elgin Groseclose, *Money and Man: A Survey of Monetary Experience* (Norman: University of Oklahoma Press), 118.

16. The Massachusetts mint was started in 1652, according to traditional sources. One might compare events in Massachusetts with those in New York State; see Lynn Ceci, "The First Fiscal Crisis in New York," *Economic and Cultural Change* 28.4 (1980): 839–47.

17. On the issues, see John J. McCusker, "Colonial Paper Money," in *Studies on Money in Early America,* ed. Eric P. Newman and Richard G. Doty (New York: American Numismatic Society, 1976), 94–104.

18. See Weeden, *Indian Money*; and Groseclose, *Money and Man.*

19. J. Earl Massey, "Early Money Substitutes," in *Studies on Money in Early America,* ed. Newman and Doty, 23.

20. See Curtis Putnam Nettels, *The Money Supply of the American Colonies before 1720* (Madison: University of Wisconsin Press, 1934).

21. Michael G. Kammen, *Colonial New York: A History* (White Plains, N.Y.: KTO Press, 1978), 162.

22. William Bradford, *Of Plymouth Plantation, 1620–47,* ed. Samuel Eliot Morison (New York: Knopf, 1966), 203.

23. The receipts for tobacco served as something like money in Virginia.

24. Berthold Fernow, "Coins and Currency of New York," in the *Memorial History of the City of New-York from Its First Settlement to the Year 1892,* ed. James Grant Wilson, 4 vols. (New York: New York History Company, 1893), 4:298.

25. Thomas Morton, *New English Canaan or New Canaan, Containing an Abstract of New England,* Charles Francis Adams (1637; repr., Boston: Printed for the [Prince] Society, 1883), 174.

26. *OED,* s.vv. "wampam, wampe."

27. *Outing: An Illustrated Monthly Magazine of Recreation 30* (1897): 367, col. 2.

28. On the sometimes ideologically crucial role of the money devil for Christendom and Christianity, see Shell, *Art and Money,* ch. 1.

29. Cooper, *Last of the Mohicans,* epigraph to ch. 30, quoting Shakespeare, *The Merchant of Venice.*

30. For an analysis of the effects of the introduction of coinage in "Asia Minor," see Shell, *Economy of Literature,* ch. 1.

31. The debate usually focuses on Alma 11.4 (in the Book of Mormon). The currency of the "Nephites" (who traveled to the New World and were utterly annihilated around A.D. 400) some say was actually wampum. See Thomas D. S. Key, *The Book of Mormon in the Light of Science,* 25th ed. (2004), http://mywebpages.comcast.net/drkey/BOM-LightofScience.pdf, accessed July 27, 2005. According to Joseph Smith, the gold plates that he discovered near Palmyra, New York, were written in "reformed Egyptian" hieroglyphic.

32. On Moses in this context, see Shell, "Moses's Tongue, in *Stutter* (Cambridge, Mass.: Harvard University Press, 2005), 102–36.

33. See Traveller Bird, *Tell Them They Lie: The Sequoyah Myth,* Great West and Indian Series 40 (Los Angeles: Westernlore, 1971), esp. 32, 83–84.

34. See Hanna Rose Shell, "Introduction: The Soul in the Skin," in William Temple Hornaday, *The*

Extermination of the American Bison, foreword by John Mack Faragher (Washington, D.C.: Smithsonian Institution Press, 2002), xiii–xxiii. Hornaday's work was first published in 1899.

35. Durand, *Some Interesting Notes,* 73. The Mohawk language, which does not have an *m* sound, names the people as *Kanien'kehá:ka.* One explanation of the name "Mohawk" is that it is a combination of two other words: the Narragansett term for "man-eaters" (*Mohowawog*) and the Unami term for "cannibal-monsters" (*Mhuweyek*).

36. For an example, see George Catlin, *Letters and Notes on the Manners, Customs, and Conditions of the North American Indians* (London: G. Catlin, 1844), letter 11.

37. The term *Indian money* is improper because wampum is not *only* money—as the term *money* is ordinarily understood. For the particular argument here, see Weeden, *Economic and Social History,*.

38. Walter Benjamin, "Tax Advice" [1926], in *Walter Benjamin: Selected Writings,* vol. 1, *1913–1926,* ed. Marcus Bullock and Michael W. Jennings (Cambridge, Mass.: Harvard University Press, 1996), 481.

39. As *Harper's* called it in an article on the American Bank Note Company: A. H. Guernsey, "Making Money," *Harper's New Monthly Magazine,* May 1862, 323.

40. An Indian overlooks a river town on a one-dollar note from Eagle Bank of Bristol, Rhode Island, 1848, *HMS* 5447). A banknote from the Mt. Pleasant and Muscatine Railway Company in Keokuk, Iowa, from the 1850s, shows Indians observing game (*HMS* 1691), and Indians hunt buffalo on the beautifully colored five-dollar note of the 1850s-60s from the Lawrence Bank in Kansas (*HMS* 1696). For the Indian seated on a tree stump with a dog, see notes from the Erie County Bank of Buffalo, New York, especially the remarkable thousand-dollar note of the 1840s (*HMS* 5510). See also the hundred-dollar bill (1840) issued by the Globe Bank of New York, reproduced in James A. Haxby, *Standard Catalog of United States Obsolete Bank Notes, 1782–1866* (Iola, Wisc.: Krause, 1988), 1625-G. This same vignette also appears on a five-dollar note of the Bank of Milwaukee, Wisconsin, in the 1830s-40s (*HMS* 5499).

41. See Fred Schwan, *Comprehensive Catalogue of Military Payment Certificates* (Port Clinton, Ohio: BNR Press, 1981), 32, 33.

Chapter 9: Wall Street and Democracy

The epigraph comes from Washington Irving, *[Diedrich Knickerbocker's] A History of New York from the Beginning of the World to the End of the Dutch Dynasty,* 3rd ed. (Philadelphia: M. Thomas, 1819), bk. 5, ch. 2. This was first published in New York by Inskeep and Bradford (1809).

1. See *Discovering America: Essays on the Search for an Identity,* ed. David Thelen and Frederick E. Hoxie (Urbana: University of Illinois Press, 1994).

2. See Elizabeth M. Black, compiler and author, *From Wampum to Wall Street: An Overview of the History of Canaan Parish* (New Canaan, Conn.: New Canaan Historical Society, 1993). "From Wampum to Wall Street" is also the name of a tour of New York City offered by Philip E. Schoenberg, president of the company New York Talks and Walks. See *From Wampum to Postal Code: The Story of the Canada Post* (Ottawa: Canada Post, 1971), an institutionally published, anonymous pamphlet that begins telling the history of the postal service in Canada with a description of "the wampum toting Iroquois and Algonkins of the pre-white man era." Coming from the Canadian postal service, the argument that there is a straight path from wampum to the Canadian postal service seems especially strange. After

all, the Canadian postal service was relatively late (1950s) even to depict Indians on its own stamps. In regard to postage stamps, see also Paul Jo Pesek, "How Stamps Portray Indians of North America," *Topical Time,* March–April 1973, 40–43.

3. See Alexander Del Mar's discussion of the use of the cacao bean in Mexico in his *History of Money in America* and elsewhere. The cacao bean's circulation as money was prohibited in Nicaragua by an executive decree dated March 29, 1869, in which that product was designated with the popular names of *moneda chilacate* and *moneda curra.* Nevertheless, it was impossible to avoid its circulation due to the lack of minted money even though the circulation of one-cent coins made in the United States had begun in 1840. See also Dr. Luis Cuadra Cea, *Aspectos historicos de la moneda en Nicaragua,* 2 vols. in 1 (Managua: Banco Central de Nicaragua, n.d.); Guillermo de la Rocha, *Breve ensayo sobre la Numismatica Nicaragua* (in *Cuadernos Universitarios,* 2nd ser., no. 18 [León, Nicaragua: Universidad Nacional Autónoma de Nicaragua, 1976], 93–117; and Dr. Ildefonso Palma Martinez, *Moneda y Bancos en Nicaragua* (Managua: Imprenta Nacional, 1975). In 1680 the *talon*—cacao—a sort of transitional measure—flourished in all parts of Central America.

4. Philip II of Spain claimed to understand nothing about "immaterial money"; see Shell, *Money, Language, and Thought,* 3.

5. See Alexander von Humboldt, *Essai politique sur le royaume de la Nouvelle Espagne* (Paris: F. Schoell, 1811). See especially his observations on the quantity of precious metals that flowed from the New World to the Old and its effect on Europe.

6. See Alexander Del Mar, *The Fluctuations of Gold* / François Grimaudet, *The Law of Payment,* trans. and ed. William Maude, 2 vols. in 1 (New York: Cambridge Encyclopedia Co., 1900).

7. Jonathan Kirshner, *Currency and Coercion: The Political Economy of International Monetary Power* (Princeton: Princeton University Press), 29, 31, quoted in Cohen, *Geography of Money,* 44.

8. Beauchamp, *Wampum and Shell Articles,* 352–54.

9. On John Law, see Shell, *Money, Language, and Thought,* 15–19.

10. Irving, *[Knickerbocker's] History of New York,* bk. 4, ch. 6, 257–58.

11. Ibid., 259, 258.

12. In Irving, *Tales of a Traveller* [by "Geoffrey Crayon, Gent."] (Philadelphia: H. C. Carey and Lea, 1824–25); "The Money-Diggers" constitutes part 4. See also "Kidd the Pirate," in the same part.

13. Irving, *[Knickerbocker's] History of New York,* bk. 5, ch. 2, 305.

14. Peter Ross, *A History of Long Island: From Its Earliest Settlement to the Present Time* (New York: Lewis, 1902), 919.

15. See Laurence M. Hauptman, "The Pequot War and Its Legacies," in *The Pequots in Southern New England: The Fall and Rise of an American Indian Nation,* ed. Laurence Hauptman and James D. Wherry, The Civilization of the American Indian Series 198 (Norman: University of Oklahoma Press, 1993), 69–80.

16. Louis Jordan, Department of Special Collections, University of Notre Dame, "Money Substitutes in New Netherland and Early New York: Wampum," http://www.coins.nd.edu/ColCoin/CoinIntros/Wampum.intro.html, accessed April 20, 2012.

17. Cornelis van Tienhoven, "Observations on the Boundary and Colonization of New Netherland," in *Documents Relative to the Colonial History of New York,* ed. O'Callaghan, 1:360; idem, "Information Respecting the Land in New Netherland," in ibid., 1:365. Van Tienhoven was writing on February 22, 1650.

18. Adriaen Cornelissen van der Donck, "Memoir on the Boundaries of New Netherland," in *Documents Relative to the Colonial History of New York,* ed. O'Callaghan, 1:458–59.

19. The treaty was signed in Hartford, Connecticut, September 29, 1650. According to a letter of Peter Stuyvesant written in 1659, the Dutch placed Oyster Bay two and a half leagues farther east than the English colonists did. In 1653, an Indian deed granted land at Oyster Bay to settlers from Massachusetts who made a permanent settlement there. In 1663, a sale was made to Captain John Underhill, who had first gone to Long Island in 1653 to lead a force in the only important engagement ever fought with the Indians on Long Island.

20. According to A. J. Chamberlain, "European-made wampum-beads affected native art in the 17th century" (*Encyclopedia Britannica* [1910], 14:470–71). On Indian methods of manufacturing wampum before the introduction of European tools, see Lewis Henry Morgan, *League of the Ho-dé-no-sau-nee or Iroquois,* ed. Herbert Marshall Lloyd, 2 vols. in 1 (New York: Dodd and Mead, 1904), 2:54–55; and Frank G. Speck and W. C. Orchid, *The Penn Wampum Belts,* foreword by George G. Heye, Leaflets of the Museum of the American Indian Heye Foundation 4 (New York: 1925), 17–20.

21. Hale, "Four Huron Wampum Records," 235.

22. Morton, *New English Canaan,* 157.

23. So suggests Davies, *History of Money,* 469.

24. The revolution itself, some have argued—among them Del Mar himself—was ultimately about money issues. See Shell, "Money Scandals," mimeographed essay at the Center for the Study of Money and Culture at Harvard University; James E. Ferguson, *The Power of the Purse: A History of American Public Finance, 1776–1790* (Chapel Hill: University of North Carolina Press, 1961); and William G. Anderson, *Price of Liberty: The Public Debt of the American Revolution* (Charlottesville: University Press of Virginia, 1983).

25. Joseph Green, *A Mournful Lamentation on the Death of Paper Money* (Wilmington, Del., 1781), quoted by Baker, *Securing the Commonwealth,* 64. See also Green's *The "Dying Speech" of Old Tenor* (Boston, 1750).

26. "Money is coined liberty, and so it is ten times dearer to the man who is deprived of freedom." Fyodor Mikhailovich Dostoevsky, *The House of the Dead* (1860–61), trans. Constance Garnett (New York: Macmillan, 1915), 16. (Different translations render the title differently.)

27. Patrick Henry, "The War Inevitable," published March 23, 1775, spoken at the Second Virginia Convention convened at St. John's Church in Richmond.

28. On the common Shakespearean pun on the terms *death* and *debt,* see Marc Shell, *The End of Kinship: "Measure for Measure," Incest, and the Ideal of Universal Kinship* (Stanford, Calif.: Stanford University Press, 1988).

29. See, for example, the three-dollar bill depicting an eagle fighting a hero, November 2, 1776. Robert H. Gore, Jr., Numismatic Endowment, University of Notre Dame.

30. See Charles Beard, *An Economic Interpretation of the Constitution of the United States* (New York: Macmillan, 1941).

31. Thomas Paine, *Common Sense* (1776), in *The Selected Work of Tom Paine,* ed. Howard Fast (New York: Duell, Sloan, and Pearce, 1945), 32. See too Davies, *History of Money,* 469.

32. See Thomas Donaldson, *The Six Nations of New York: Cayugas, Mohawks (Saint Regis), Oneidas, Onondagas, Senecas, Tuscaroras. Report of Indians Taxed and not Taxed* (Washington, D.C.: Government Printing Office, 1894).

33. This belt is example 244 in Beauchamp, *Wampum and Shell Articles Used*.

34. *Minutes of the Provincial Council of Pennsylvania: From the Organization to the Termination of the Proprietary Government*, 10 vols. (Harrisburg, Pa.: 1851–52), 1:586; see Merrell, *Into the American Woods*, 191.

35. Merrell, *Into the American Woods*, 191 (quotation), 192.

36. Washington quoted in Gregory Schaaf, *Wampum Belts and Peace Trees: George Morgan, Native Americans, and Revolutionary Diplomacy* (Golden, Colo.: Fulcrum Publishing, 1990), xx ("A united force"); George Washington to Major General Philip Schuyler, Cambridge, January 27, 1776, in *The Writings of George Washington from the Original Manuscript Sources, 1745–1799*, ed. John Fitzpatrick, 38 vols. (Washington, D.C.: Government Printing Office, 1931–44), 4:280, quoted in Schaaf, *Wampum Belts and Peace Trees*, 8 ("a little embarrassed").

37. Quoted by Merrell, *Into the American Woods*, 188.

38. See Hezekiah Butterworth, *The Wampum Belt, or The Fairest Page of History: A Tale of William Penn's Treaty with the Indians* (New York: Appleton, 1924).

39. Schaaf, *Wampum Belts and Peace Trees*, 116, 118, 121, 151, 157, 179. On the term *wampum diplomacy* and what it means, see Paul A. Wallace, *Indians in Pennsylvania* (Harrisburg: Pennsylvania Historical Society and Museum Commission, 1968), 53–55.

40. Schaaf, *Wampum Belts and Peace Trees*, 21, quoting from the Morgan Papers.

41. Ibid., 53.

42. Ibid., 68.

43. Merrell, *Into the American Woods*, 192. For these lettered belts, Merrell quotes *Minutes of the Provincial Council of Pennsylvania*.

44. "Whatever their design and their message, shells were a go-between's stock in trade. He advised wampum makers on the size, color, and pattern of belts, kept beads on hand just in case, and, before setting out with a message, packed hundreds, even thousands of the shells among the 'nessecarys . . . to Facilitate the Success of his Journey.' To run short or run out was to court disaster. [Conrad] Weiser fretted that one emissary bound for the Indian countries 'was without wampum for accidents,' and in February 1760 Teedyuscung, preparing for another trip, complained 'that he has not got Wampum enough" to carry Pennsylvania's words of peace.'" Ibid., 192.

45. This nineteenth-century thesis from such writers as William E. Griffs (*Sir William Johnson and the Six Nations* [New York: Dodd and Mead, 1891]) was taken up in the 1990s by Donald A. Grinde Jr. and Bruce E. Johansen in their *Exemplar of Liberty: Native America and the Evolution of Democracy*, foreword by Vine Deloria (Los Angeles: American Studies Center, 1991). See also Mark Openheimer, "Field Notes: Tribal Lore," *Lingua Franca*, March 1997. 8–9. In this vein, in the Iroquois *Akwesasne Notes* (3.3 [Midwinter 1992]), we read: "In 1755 . . . at the 'Albany Congress,' we suggested to twelve British colonies that they should form a union, for strength and peace." Quoted in Martien, *Shell Game*, 113n. On the other hand, there have always been those who have denied the likelihood of such an influence. (For the contemporary denial of real influence, see the *William and Mary Quarterly*, July 1996, esp. the statements of Philip Levy and Samuel Payne Jr.) Concerning the age of the confederacy, it has been argued recently that it dates back to A.D. 1142. Bruce E. Johansen, "Dating the Iroquois Confederacy," *Akwesasne Notes*, n.s., 1:3–4 (Fall 1995): 62–63, repr., *Crazy Horse Spirit*, January–February 1996, the newsletter of the Leonard Peltier Defense Committee. It appears that Benjamin Franklin read Cadwallader Colden's work *The history of the Five Nations of Canada, . . . with accounts of their . . . forms of government* (London: T. Osborne, 1747) and then visited Colden before, and by way of preparation

for, drawing up his Albany Plan of Union (1754). Colden, who was an adopted Mohawk, had essayed to demonstrate that, among the Iroquois, "each nation is an absolute Republick by its self, governed in all affairs of war and peace by the sachems of old men, whose authority and power is gained by and consists wholly in the opinions of the rest of the Nation in their wisdom and integrity" (17). He served as the first colonial representative to the Iroquois Confederacy and was acting governor of New York (1760–62 and then, with a short break, 1763–65) and then its governor (1769–71).

46. Woody West, "The Way West: Series' PC Myth-making Turns Indians into Saints and Whites into Savages," *Washington Time,* May 7, 1995, a review of CBS's *500 Nations,* Turner Broadcasting's *The Native Americans,* the Discovery Channel's *How the West Was Lost,* and the PBS series *The Way West.*

47. Martien, *Shell Game,* 108.

48. See Gerald R. Alfred, *Heeding the Voices of Our Ancestors: Kahnawake Mohawk Politics and the Rise of Native Nationalism* (Toronto: Oxford University Press, 1995). Alfred also calls the Iroquois Confederacy "the first genuine North American federal system" (78). Kevin Costner's *500 Nations*—an eight-hour documentary aired in four segments on CBS during spring 1995—suggested that Benjamin Franklin was influenced by Haudenosaunee government. Sally Roesch Wagner, in "Is Equality Indigenous? The Untold Iroquois Influence on Early Feminists," *On the Issues* (Winter 1996): 21–25, discusses how some anglophone American women in the nineteenth century considered that the relations between the genders might be transformed by studying matrilineal aspects of the confederation.

49. Peña, "Wampum Production," 33, tells of a day when Hiawatha was resting by a lake: "When the ducks on the lake flew away, the lake bottom was revealed to be covered with white shells which Hiawatha collected and strung. Another version of the myth describes a bird from the Other World who was coated with wampum. A local chief offered the hand of his daughter in exchange for this bird. Eventually a youth from an enemy tribe killed the bird and married the chief's daughter. He divided the wampum between his tribe and his wife's, making peace between the two and establishing the use of wampum as a peacemaker." See also Longfellow, *Hiawatha.* Concerning wampum and the confederacy: the legends of the Iroquois suggest that the original wampum beads date from around 1570, when the confederation was established. The Mi'kmaq work I was assigned to study when a student at Algonquin school in Montréal confirms this.

50. Henry Rowe Schoolcraft, *The Myth of Hiawatha and Other Oral Legends Mythologic and Allegoric of the North American Indians* (Philadelphia and London: J. B. Lippincott and Trubner, 1856), 14. For Hiawatha as founder of the Iroquois Confederacy, see Lynn Ceci, "The Value of Wampum among the New York Iroquois: A Case Study in Artifact Analysis," *Journal of Archaeological Research* 38.1 (Spring 1982): 97–107 (quote on 102–3).

51. Franklin studied the Iroquois Confederacy and wrote and spoke on the idea of building a colonial confederation similar to that of the Iroquois.

52. One story has it that when, in February 1776, Benjamin Franklin began to design money for the emerging American nation, he used Iroquois covenant chain imagery, especially when coming to the new "Two[-]Thirds of a Dollar." This bill eventually depicted an emblem of the thirteen colonies interlocked in a continuous chain of unity. A motto asserted "American Congress, We are one." The same design appears on American coinage in 1787. The grand sachem of the Tammany society wore a silver chain with thirteen links after the American Revolution. See Ron Wellburn, "The Great Seal of the United States: Esoteric Parallel to the Iroquois Influence-Constitution Debate," *Roanoke and Wampum: Topics in Native American Heritage and Literatures* (New York: Peter Lang, 2001), 51–68.

53. See Franklin, *A Modest Enquiry into the Nature and Necessity of a Paper-Currency* (Philadelphia: Printed and sold [by Benjamin Franklin] at the new printing-office, near the market, 1729). As a printer, Franklin was involved not only in making money in the sense of earning a profit but also in making money in the sense of creating the material object that is paper money.

54. Franklin, *A Copy of a Letter from Quebeck in Canada to a pr—e-m—r in France, dated October 11, 1747* (United States: s.n., 1747), 4 pages, microform (Lamont Library, Harvard University). This publication was ascribed to the press of Benjamin Franklin by Charles Evans in the earlier part of the twentieth century in *Early American Imprints*, 1st ser, no. 5925 (New Canaan, Conn.: Readex; Worcester, Mass.: American Antiquarian Society, 2002). However, this attribution is refuted by Clarence William Miller in *Benjamin Franklin's Philadelphia Printing, 1728–1766: A Descriptive Bibliography* (Philadelphia: American Philosophical Society, 1974), B44.

55. Thomas Jefferson, letter sent from Paris, December 15, 1786, in *The Life and Selected Writings of Thomas Jefferson* ed. Adrienne Koch and William Peden (New York: Modern Library, 1944), 378.

56. See Howard McLellan, "Indian Magna Carta Writ in Wampum Belts: Six Nations Shows Treaty Granting Them Independent Sovereignty as Long as Sun Shines," *New York Times,* June 7, 1925.

57. See Tehanetorens, "The Formation of the Hodenosaune or League of the Five Nations," in *Tales of the Iroquois* (Ohswekan, Ont., Can.: Iroqrafts, 1992); originally published in Rooseveltown, New York, in *Akwasasne Notes* (1976) (Six Nations Museum series publication). See also Richard White, *The Middle Ground: Indians, Empires, and Republics in the Great Lakes Region, 1650–1815* (Cambridge: Cambridge University Press, 1991).

58. See Cadwallader Colden, *The History of the Five Indian Nations Depending on the Province of New-York in America* (New York: William Bradford, 1727); reprinted as *Early American Imprints*, 1st ser. no. 2849.

59. Smith, *Generall Historie of Virginia,* 47; the word appears there as *Caw-cawwassoughes.*

60. Trumbull, *On Some Words Derived from Languages of North American Indians,* 11.

61. George Campbell, *White and Black: The Outcome of a Visit to the United States* (New York: R. Worthington, 1879), 63.

62. See, for example, Sandra Joyce Pflug, "The Iroquois Wampum Belt as a Cultural Metaphor" (master's thesis, Trent University, Peterborough, Ont., May 1992).

63. Benson J. Lossing, *Our Country: A Household History for All Readers, from the Discovery of America to the One hundredth Anniversary of the Declaration of Independence,* illus. Felix O. C. Darley, 3 vols. (New York: Johnson Wilson, 1875–78): 1:440.

64. Emerson, "The Poet," in *Essays and English Traits,* 176.

65. Henry Noel Humphreys, *The Coin Manual; or, Guide to the Numismatic Student in the Formation of a Cabinet of Coins* (London: Bohn, 1853), 1:217.

66. Kenneth Malcolm MacKenzie, *Countermarks of the Ottoman Empire, 1880–1922* (Sanderstead, Surrey, U.K.: Hawkins Publications, 1974).

67. On Greek coins, see C. J. Howgego, *Greek Imperial Countermarks: Studies in the Provincial Coinage of the Roman Empire,* Royal Numismatic Society 17 (London: Royal Numismatic Society, 1985). For issues from Akragas, see Luigi Pedroni, *Le contromarche di Akragas* (Napoli: Liguori, 1995). Roman imperial coins are discussed in Peter Kos and Andrej Šemrov, *Rimski novci in kontramarke iz 1. stoletja: Augustus–Traianus* (Roman imperial coins and countermarks of the first century: Augustus to Trajan), Situla 33, Zbirka Numizmaticnega kabineta Narodnega muzeja (The collection of the Numismatic Cabinet of

the National Museum) 2 (Ljubljana, Slovenia: Narodny muzej, 1995). For Byzantine coins, see N. M. Lowick, *The Mardin Hoard: Islamic Countermarks on Byzantine Folles* (London: A. H. Baldwin, 1977).

68. See Mayer Rosenberger, *The Coinage of Eastern Palestine and Legionary Countermarks, Bar-Kochba Overstrucks* (Jerusalem: Rosenberger, 1978).

69. Certain ironies in the notion of "assimilation" as such are considered in Frederick E. Hoxie, *A Final Promise: The Campaign to Assimilate the Indians, 1880–1920,* with new pref. (Lincoln: University of Nebraska Press, 2001).

Chapter 10: What Happened to Wampum

The chapter's opening epigraphs are from Wood, "Small Nomenclator," 118; and Calvin Coolidge, address to the American Society of Newspaper Editors, Washington, D.C., January 17, 1925. That is how Calvin Coolidge's words are usually reported. According to the written record, however, he actually said, "The chief business of the American people is business." Coolidge, *Foundations of the Republic: Speeches and Addresses* (New York: Scribner, 1926), 187. The epigraph following the subhead "Knowing Who's Who" is from Augustus H. van Buren, *A History of Ulster County under the Dominion of the Dutch* (Kingston, N.Y.: privately printed, 1923), 35. The epigraph following the subhead "Roanoke, and How" is from Henry C. Watson, *The Yankee Tea-Party; or, Boston in 1773* (Philadelphia: Lindsay and Blakiston, 1851), 104.

1. See the discussion in Charles L. Cutler, *O Brave New Words! Native American Loanwords in Current English* (Norman: University of Oklahoma Press, 1994).

2. Thomas Anburey, *Travels through the Interior Parts of America: In a Series of Letters* (London: W. Lane, 1789), 2:50. Anburey says that the Virginians applied this term to the inhabitants of New England for not assisting the Virginians in a war with the Cherokees. *OED,* s.v. "Yankee."

3. Heckewelder, *History, Manners, and Customs of the Indian Nations,* 77n4. There are several other probable etymologies.

4. The term has a long history: "[They] are considered capable of 'Yankeeing' the more simple-minded Canadians." *Fraser's Magazine* 16 (1837): 683. *To gyp,* from *Gypsy,* and *to jew,* from *Jew,* work in much the same way.

5. The term *glottophagia* comes from the Greek terms *phago,* meaning "eat," and *glottis,* meaning "tongue"; *glottophagia* is far less common in English than other languages. See C. Bierbach, "Zwischen Humanismus und Glottophagie: Die Sprachenfrage in der Eroberung der Neuen Welt (am Beispiel Mexico)," in *Sprachgeschichte und Soziolinguistik: Querverbindungen,* ed. C. Bierbach and G. Berkenbusch (Tübingen: Narr, 1994), 11–129; and, above all, Louis-Jean Calvet, *Linguistique et colonialisme: Petit traite de glottophagie* (Paris: Éditions Payot, 1974).

6. Daniel H. Usner, "Iroquois Livelihood and Jeffersonian Agrarianism," in Hoxie et al., *Native Americans,* 201.

7. James Gilchrist, *The Etymologic Interpreter or Dictionary of the English Language* (London: R. Hunter, 1824), 8.

8. See Laurier Turgeon, "Le sens de l'objet interculturel: la ceinture de wampum," in *Entre Beauce et l'Acadie: Facettes d'un parcours ethnologique. Études offertes au professeur Jean-Claude Dupont,* ed. Turgeon (Québec: Les Presses de l'Université Laval, 2001), 136–52.

9. Alvin E. Rust, *Mormon and Utah Coin and Currency* (Salt Lake City: Rust Rare Coin Co., 1984), 160–61 (see figure 206); Theodore Roosevelt, *Presidential Addresses and State Papers,* 8 vols. (New York: Review of Reviews, 1910), 8:2011–12.

10. Q. David Bowers, *A Guide Book of Buffalo and Jefferson Nickels* (Atlanta: Whitman, 2007), 38–39; on the sculptor James Earle Fraser, see A. L. Freundlich, *The Sculpture of James Earle Fraser* (Boca Raton, Fla.: Universal, 2001).

11. Hale, "Four Huron Wampum Records," 233.

12. Ibid., 234.

13. Anne Stearns Baker Molloy, *Wampum* (New York: Hastings House, 1977). This children's book is listed as an official "resource book" by the Onondaga Nation.

14. In recent decades there has been a great deal of interest in returning wampum to various Indian groups and individuals. See, among other sources, New York Education Department, "Wampum Belts Returned to the Onandaga Nation," *Man in the Northeast* 38 (Fall 1989): 109–17; Elisabeth Tooker, "A Note on the Return of Eleven Wampum Belts to the Six Nations Iroquois Confederacy on Grand River, Canada," *Ethnohistory* 45.2 (1998): 219–36; José Barreiro, "Return of the Wampum," *Northeast Indian Quarterly* 7.1 (Spring 1990): 8–20. See also Martin Sullivan, "Return of the Sacred Wampum Belts of the Iroquois," *The History Teacher* 26.1 (1992) 7–14.

15. "Ce qu'était le 'wampum,'" *Bulletin des recherches historiques* 31 (1925): 296–97.

16. The *OED* suggests that *mask* and *mascot* share a common etymon: the postclassical *masca* (*OED,* s.vv. "mask" and "mascot").

17. "The art [of wampum-making] soon fell into disuse, however; for wampum better than their own was brought them by the traders, besides abundant imitations in glass and porcelain." Parkman, *France and England in North America,* part 2, *France and England in North America,* xxxi–xxxii.

18. Hale, "Four Wampum Records," 228.

19. On the so-called Vatican Wampum Belt, see Marshall Joseph Becker, "The Vatican Wampum Belt: An Important American Indian Artifact and Its Cultural Origins and Meaning within the Category of 'Religious' or 'Ecclesiastical-Convert' Belts," *Bolletino, Monumenti Musei e Gallerie Pontificie* 21 (2001): 363–411.

20. See, for example, Beauchamp, *Wampum and Shell Articles,* 390–91.

21. *Pennsylvania Archives, 1664–1790,* ed. Samuel Hazard, ser. 1 (Philadelphia: J. Severns, 1852–56), 8:217, quoted in Beauchamp, *Wampum and Shell Articles,* 391. I added the italics and square brackets but not the contents of the latter.

22. Emily Pauline Johnson (Tekahionwake), *Collected Poems and Selected Prose,* ed. Carole Gerson and Veronica Strong-Boag (Toronto: University of Toronto Press, 2002), 115.

23. *The Poetical Works of Mrs. Leprohon* (Miss Rosanna Eleanor Mullins) (Montréal: J. Lovell, 1881), 68.

24. John (Fire) Lame Deer and Richard Erdoes, *Lame Deer, Seeker of Visions* (New York: Simon and Schuster, 1972), 42. This concerns the Teton Indians.

25. See John Canfield Ewers, *The Blackfeet: Raiders on the Northwestern Plains* (Norman: University of Oklahoma Press, 1958), 200–201. See also Ewers, *Plains Indian History and Culture: Essays on Continuity and Change* (Norman: University of Oklahoma Press, 1958), 55.

26. Gilbert W. Hagerty, *Wampum, War, and Trade Goods West of the Hudson* (Interlaken, N.Y.: Heart of the Lake Publishing, 1985), 203 ("The chief laughed), 204 ("The Indians thought").

27. The Chinese of the Yellow River valley in the eighth century B.C. had similar monetary tokens.

Their diminutive "knife money" was exchangeable for regular-size knives as well as for other goods. François Thierry, "The Origins and Development of Chinese Coins," in *Origin, Evolution and Circulation of Foreign Coins in the Indian Ocean*, ed. Osmund Bopearachchi and D. P. M. Weerakkody (New Delhi: Manohar, 1998), 15–62.

28. On reducing to a silver base, see William Fenton, *The Great Law and the Longhouse: A Political History of the Iroquois Confederacy* (Norman: University of Oklahoma Press, 1998), 227. Stuyvesant quoted in *Documents Relative to the Colonial History of New York,* ed. O'Callaghan, vol. 14, ed. Berthold Fernow, 470, quoted by Fenton, *Great Law,* 227 ("Wampum is the source").

29. Weeden, *Indian Money,* 15. For Vima Kadphises (circa A.D. 100–127/8), see Michael Mitchiner, *Oriental Coins and Their Values,* vol. 2, *The Ancient and Classical World* (London: Hawkins Publications, 1978), 3033–35 (Gobl Kushan 762).

30. William Martin Beauchamp, *Metallic Ornaments of the New York Indians,* New York State Museum Bulletin 73 (Albany: University of the State of New York, 1903), 45.

31. Cooper, *Last of the Mohicans,* ch. 30, 392.

32. Hagerty, *Wampum, War and Trade Goods,* 301, mentioned coins and coin hoards at Oak Hill, or Tionontoguen, where silver coins of Dutch origin were often traded.

33. See Nicolas Benjamin Doucet, *Fundamental Principles of the Laws of Canada, as they existed under the natives, as they were changed under the French kings, and as they were modified and altered under the domination of England* (Montréal: J. Lovell, 1841–47). In Canada, Parliament was called upon to regulate the importation of wampum even in the nineteenth century. Such importation was necessary in order to allow the Indians to trade, according to the Act to Permit the Importation of Wampum, from the Neighboring States by the Inland Communication of Lake Champlain, and the River Richelieu or Sorel, Provincial Parliament of Lower Canada, 1792.

34. July 17, 1709, document 67, in Ives Goddard and Kathleen J. Bragdon, *Native Writings in Massachusett,* 2 vols. (Philadelphia: American Philosophical Society, 1988), 1:230–33.

35. The Indians used hair pipes "in intertribal trade long before the first white trader appeared among them." Ewers, "Hair Pipes," 73.

36. Ewers, "Hair Pipes," 37. "For nearly two centuries, white men who have traded with the Indians of the Eastern Woodlands and the Great Plains have referred to a tubular bead measuring 1½ inches or more in length which they carried in stock by the name of 'hair pipe'" (ibid.). The first recorded uses of the term *hair pipe* or *hair bob* by anglophone traders comes from George Morgan and others who were in the Ohio Valley in the 1760s ordering silver hair pipes (and/or hair bobs), according to Ewers (ibid., 37, 40). See too Harrold E. Gillingham, "Indian Silver Ornaments," *Pennsylvania Magazine of History and Biography* 58.2 (1934): 97–126; and idem, *Indian Ornaments Made by Philadelphia Silversmiths* (New York: Museum of the American Indian, Heye Foundation, 1936).

37. "The so-called Mobilian trade language was a corrupted Choctaw jargon used for the purposes of inter-tribal communication among all the tribes from Florida to Louisiana, extending northward on the Mississippi to about the junction of the Ohio. It was also known as the Chickasaw trade language." Frederick Webb Hodge, ed., *Handbook of American Indians North of Mexico,* 2 vols. (Washington, D.C.: Government Printing Office, 1907), 1:916, col. 1. On Choctaw in general as a trading language, see James Crawford, *The Mobilian Trade Language* (Knoxville: University of Tennessee Press, 1978).

38. On the now multilingual term *OK*—and also on its purported multilingual etymologies—see Shell, *The Painting in the Trash Bin* (forthcoming).

39. "Scaiohady & the half King, with two others, had inform'd me that they often must send Messengers to Indian Towns & Nations, & had nothing in their Council Bag, as they were new beginners, either to recompense a Messenger or to get Wampum to do the business, & begged I wou'd assist them with something." Conrad Weiser's journal entry written in Pennsbury, Pennsylvania, September 29, 1748, in *Conrad Weiser's Journal of a Tour to the Ohio, August 11-October 2, 1748,* repr. in *Early Western Travels, 1748–1846,* vol. 1, ed. Reuben Gold Thwaites (Cleveland, Ohio: A. H. Clark, 1904), 15–44.

40. The relevant passage from Bradford's *Of Plymouth Foundation* is quoted in chapter 8.

41. On the shell in that geographical area, see John Lawson, *A New Voyage to Carolina: Containing the exact description and natural history of that country* (London, 1709), 204–5, quoted in Fred Willard, "Trade Items as Transfers of Money," honors thesis for East Carolina University Honors Program, November 2002. Regarding the early use of shell, see David L. Bushnell Jr., "Virginia—From Early Records," *American Anthropologist* 9.1 (January–March 1907): 31–44. Bushnell describes early "ethnological specimens from Virginia" at the Ashmolean Museum, at Oxford, including early seventeenth-century wampum beadwork that he believes to be the oldest example of North American beadwork and "additional proof of the prehistoric origin of wampum" (40). The Nanticoke Indians (from around Chesapeake Bay), who traded around Roanoke, were sometimes reported to be "money changers" or bankers of Indian shell money; see Raphael Semmes, *Captains and Mariners of Early Maryland* (Baltimore: Johns Hopkins University Press, 1937). John Smith wrote of them: "Here [the Chesapeake] doth inhabite the people Sarapinagh, Nause, Arseek, and Nantaquak, the best Marchants of all other Salvages." Smith, *Generall Historie of Virginia,* 118.

42. See William Edward Fitch, *The First Founders in America, with facts to prove that Sir Walter Raleigh's lost colony was not lost, a paper read at a stated meeting of the New York Society of the Order of the Founders and Patriots of America, held at the Hotel Manhattan, October 29, A.D. 1913* (New York: The Society, 1913, 59).

43. See Thomas Hariot, *A Briefe and True Report of the New Found Land of Virginia: Of the Commodities and of the Nature and Manners of the Naturall Inhabitants: Discouered bÿ the English Colonÿ There Seated by Sir Richard Greinuile Knight In the Yeere 1585,* trans. [from Latin] Richard Hakluyt (London, 1588); see also the edition ill. John White and engr. Theodor de Bry (Frankfurt, 1588).

44. Stefan Lorant, *The New World: The First Pictures of America, Made by John White and Jacques Le Moyne and Engraved by Theodore de Bry, with Contemporary Narratives of the French Settlements in Florida, 1562–1565, and the English Colonies in Virginia, 1585–1590,* rev. ed. (New York: Duell, Sloan, and Pearce 1965).

45. See James Phinney Baxter, "Raleigh's Lost Colony," *New England Magazine* (1895), 565–85; David N. Durant, *Raleigh's Lost Colony* (New York: Atheneum, 1981); David B. Quinn, *The Lost Colonists: Their Fortune and Probable Fate* (Raleigh: America's Four Hundredth Anniversary Committee, North Carolina Department of Cultural Resources, 1984); Karen Ordahl Kupperman, *Roanoke: The Abandoned Colony* (Totowa, N.J.: Rowman and Allanheld, 1984).

46. George Chapman et al., *Eastward Hoe: As it was Playd in the Black-friers. By the Children of her Maiesties Reuels* (London: Printed [by George Eld] for William Aspley, 1605). *Eastward Hoe* refers to the colonists left in America. For reference to Roanoke as a mystery, see Lee Miller, *Roanoke: Solving the Mystery of England's Lost Colony* (London: Jonathan Cape, 2000). Melvin Robinson terms the situation a riddle in *Riddle of the Lost Colony* (New Bern, N.C.: Owen G. Dunn, 1946), whereas it is an enigma in Jean Carl Harrington, *Archaeology and the Enigma of Fort Raleigh* (Raleigh: North Carolina Department of Cultural Resources, 1984). On Green's work, see Lamar Stringfield, *The Lost Colony Song-Book: Songs, Hymns, Dances and Other Music from the Play, "The Lost Colony" by Paul Green,* compiled

and collected, with additional lyrics, by Paul Green; special music by Lamar Stringfield; additional settings by Lamar Stringfield and Adeline McCall (New York: C. Fischer, 1938). In addition, see the earlier work by Stephen Beauregard Weeks, *The Lost Colony of Roanoke: Its Fate and Survival* (New York: Knickerbocker Press, 1891).

47. See, for example, Harrington, *Archaeology and the Enigma of Fort Raleigh;* E. Thomson Shields and Charles Robin Ewen, eds., *Searching for the Roanoke Colonies: An Interdisciplinary Collection* (Raleigh: North Carolina Department of Cultural Resources, Office of Archives and History, 2003).

48. Bryce Nelson, "Lost Colony?" *Atlanta Journal and Constitution,* May 15, 1977, 10-B.

49. See Lew Barton, *The Most Ironic Story in American History: An Authoritative, Documented History of the Lumbee Indians of North Carolina,* photo. Elmer Hunt (Pembroke, N.C.: the author, 1967).

50. Smith, *Generall Historie of Virginia,* 121.

51. George and Ira Gershwin, "They All Laughed," from the movie *Shall We Dance* (1937).

52. See *OED,* s.v. "ho," int. 1, n. 2.

53. *OED,* s.v. "how," int. 1, n. 4. On the use of the American term(s) to indicate approval of a speech, see Jean de Brébeuf, writing in the seventeenth century, in *The Jesuit Relations and Allied Documents . . . 1610–1791,* ed. Reuben Gold Thwaites, 73 vols. (Cleveland: Burrows Bros., 1886–1901), 10:259. See also *OED,* s.v. "how," int. 2.

54. Ohiyesa [Charles Alexander Eastman], "My Plays and Playmates I: Games and Sports," *Indian Boyhood,* ill. E. L. Blumenschein (New York: McClure, Phillips, 1902), 70–71. Eastman was a Santee Sioux.

55. See Elaine Goodale Eastman, *Sister to the Sioux,* ed. Kay Graber (Lincoln: University of Nebraska Press, 1978); and Charles B. Ewing, "The Wounded of the Wounded Knee Battlefield," *Boston Medical and Surgical Journal* (May 12, 1892): 36–56. On the Ghost Dance, see James Mooney, "The Ghost-Dance Religion and the Sioux Outbreak of 1890," *Smithsonian Institution, Bureau of American Ethnology, Annual Report* [Washington, D.C.] 14.2 (1896).

56. *Whoop* was often used to describe Indian-language "sounds," as when the influential historian Francis Parkman writes, "An Indian chief . . . ran to meet them, whooping and clamoring welcome." Parkman, *France and England in North America,* part 1, *Pioneers of France in the New World* (Boston: Little, Brown, 1880), section 1, "Huguenots in Florida," 44.

INDEX

requirement for trade, 58–60; semiotic syncretism, 91–93; terms for, 36–37, 48, 98, 108nn5–6, 109n8, 128n41; as type of scripture, 39; uses of, 1–2, 11–12, 42, 109nn9, 110n2; vilification of, 63; wearing of, 102n2; as writing, 113n13, 115n35

Wampum, Pa., 66

Wampum, War, and Trade Goods (Hagerty), 94

Wampum Belt, The (Butterworth), 81

wampum belts: European and Colonial style belts, 39–41, *40–41*; Four Nations Alliance belt, *53*; friendship belts, *52*, *54*; League Belt, *40*, 41; Penn Belt, *39*; Penobscot marriage belt, *49*; ransom belt, *43*; religious, 90–91, *91–92*; repatriation of, 90; Simcoe belt, *41*; tribal belt, *40*

wampum keeper (*hiawatha*), 56, 90, 116n53

Wampum Treaty ("The Holy Experiment"), 81

Wamsutta, Chief, 33

Wapapi Akonutomakonol, 49

Washington, George, 41, 77, 81

Washington Covenant Belt, 39, *40*, 110n24

Watson, Henry C., 97

Weeden, William, 2, 66, 94

Weetamo, Queen (Pocasset), 30

Weiser, Conrad, 97, 122n44, 128n39

Welch, Samuel Manning, 19

wen (China), 13, 105n14

What Cheer (Durfee), 29

what cheer netop (greetings), 28–29, 107n15

"What 'Wampum' Was" (*Bulletin des recherches historiques*), 90–93

White, John, 97–98

White Maiden and the Indian Girl, The (Lephrohon), 93

White Wampum, The (E. Johnson), 93

Whorf, Benjamin, 55, 96

Williams, Roger, 22, 29, 35

Willie Wampum (Marquette University mascot), 45

"Wing or Dust Fan of the President of Six Nations" (wampum belt), 81

"Wolfert Webber" (Irving), 75

Wood, William, 35, 36, 43, 87

Woodward, Samuel P., 36

written language, 55

Wynadot ("people of one speech"), 6

"yankee," 4, 125nn2

MARC SHELL is Irving Babbitt Professor of Comparative Literature and professor of English at Harvard University. He is the author of many books, including *The Economy of Literature*; *Money, Language, and Thought*; and *Art and Money*.

The University of Illinois Press
is a founding member of the
Association of American University Presses.

———————————————

Designed by Kelly Gray
Composed in 11.25/14 Perpetua
by Jim Proefrock
at the University of Illinois Press
Manufactured by Sheridan Books, Inc.

University of Illinois Press
1325 South Oak Street
Champaign, IL 61820-6903
www.press.uillinois.edu